BREAKING FREE
FROM OCD

BREAKING FREE
FROM OCD

A CBT Guide for Young People and Their Families

Jo Derisley, Isobel Heyman, Sarah Robinson
and Cynthia Turner

Illustrated by Lisa Jo Robinson

Jessica Kingsley *Publishers*
London and Philadelphia

Throughout this book the authors use case examples which are based on real clinical cases.
Every effort has been made to change the identity of the people involved.
The authors would like to thank all of the children, adolescents and parents we have worked with
who have given us the opportunity to write such real and rich case examples.

First published in 2008
by Jessica Kingsley Publishers
73 Collier Street
London N1 9BE, UK
and
400 Market Street, Suite 400
Philadelphia, PA 19106, USA

www.jkp.com

Library of Congress Cataloging in Publication Data

**Breaking free from OCD : a CBT guide for young people and their families / Jo Derisley ...
[et al.]. -- 1st American pbk. ed.**
    p. cm.
    **ISBN 978-1-84310-574-9 (pb : alk. paper) 1. Obsessive-compulsive disorder in adoles-
cence--Popular works. I. Derisley, Jo.**
    RJ506.O25B74 2008
    618.92'85227--dc22

                                        2007051738

British Library Cataloguing in Publication Data
A CIP catalogue record for this book is available from the British Library

ISBN 978 1 84310 574 9
eISBN 978 1 84642 799 2

CONTENTS

PART A: Understanding Your OCD

Chapter 1: About this Book   13

Why should I read this book?; How should I use this book?;
What are the treatments for OCD?; Summary

Advice for parents or carers: Recommended treatments

Chapter 2: What is OCD?   19

So what is OCD?; The various symptoms of OCD; Some
information about your thoughts; Do I have OCD?; Summary

Advice for parents or carers: What is obsessive compulsive
disorder?; Does my child have OCD?; Why does my child
have OCD?

Chapter 3: Can I Get Better from OCD?   31

How to get help; What are the treatments for OCD?; How do
we know treatments work?; Summary

Advice for parents or carers: Getting help for your child with
OCD; What if my child does not want help?; What
assessment will the doctor do, and what treatments will be
recommended?

Chapter 4: What is Cognitive Behaviour Therapy?   40

Cognitive behaviour therapy (CBT) for OCD; Some facts
about CBT for OCD; Summary

Advice for parents or carers

Chapter 5: Understanding My OCD   **46**

Understanding your obsessions and compulsions; The OCD trap; How does *your* OCD trap work?; Drawing your own OCD trap; What does OCD make me avoid?; What would life be like without OCD?; Summary

Advice for parents or carers: Your child's obsessions and compulsions; How has OCD affected the family?

PART B: How to Recover from Your OCD

Chapter 6: How to Use this Book to Change Your OCD   **61**

Measuring your OCD; Summary

Advice for parents or carers: How to help; Summary

Chapter 7: Understanding the Role of Anxiety   **69**

What is anxiety?; The physical effects of anxiety; When is anxiety helpful?; When is anxiety unhelpful?; Can anxiety harm me?; Habituation or 'getting used to' anxiety; An 'anxiety thermometer'; Using an 'anxiety thermometer' to rate how you feel about doing a task; Using an 'anxiety thermometer' to rate how you feel over time; Anxiety graphs; Summary

Advice for parents or carers

Chapter 8: What does My OCD Look Like?   **80**

What are my OCD problems?; Keeping an OCD diary; Making an OCD ladder; Deciding where to start; What should I do next?; Summary

Advice for parents or carers: Summary

Chapter 9: Designing Exposure and Response Prevention Exercises   **94**

What is exposure and response prevention (E/RP)?; Designing your first E/RP exercise; Learning to break OCD's rules; Doing your first E/RP exercise; Updating your OCD ladder; What should I do next?; Summary

Advice for parents or carers: Summary

Chapter 10: Making Progress with Exposure and Response Prevention Exercises   **110**

How to do more exposure and response prevention (E/RP) exercises; Making sense of your findings; What to do if you get stuck; What should I do if others are involved in my OCD?; What should I do next?; Summary

Advice for parents or carers: When OCD involves you; How to withdraw from OCD's demands; What to do about reassurance seeking; Summary

Chapter 11: Overcoming Difficulties   **120**

Questions and answers; What should I do next?; Summary

Advice for parents or carers: Summary

Chapter 12: What Is the Role of My Thoughts?   **132**

How important are your thoughts?; What are typical OCD thoughts?; Thinking helpful thoughts; What to say to OCD; How to think helpful thoughts; More about fighting back with helpful thoughts; What should I do next?; Summary

Advice for parents or carers: Summary

Chapter 13: How Can I Challenge My Thoughts?   **147**

Learning to put OCD worries on trial; How to make a responsibility pie-chart; What should I do next?; Summary

Advice for parents or carers: When obsessional thoughts involve you; Summary

Chapter 14: How Can I Test Whether My Thoughts Will Come True?   **159**

What is a behavioural experiment?; Why should I do behavioural experiments?; How do behavioural experiments work?; How to carry out a behavioural experiment; How to overcome problems with behavioural experiments; What should I do next?; Check your progress; Summary

Advice for parents or carers: How to help your child understand his or her beliefs; Summary

Chapter 15: How to Maintain the Gains I Have Made   **173**

When might OCD try to reappear?; What might OCD look like if it tries to reappear?; What other things can I do?; What goals do I have for my life?; Summary

Advice for parents or carers

PART C: OCD and the Bigger Picture

Chapter 16: OCD and My Family   187

How does OCD affect families?; You *can* overcome OCD;
Frequently asked questions (FAQs)

Advice for parents or carers

Chapter 17: OCD, School and Friends   196

OCD and school; OCD and your friends; Telling your friends
about OCD

Chapter 18: Where to Go for More Information   201

Books for young people; Books for children; Books for
parents or carers; Websites

APPENDIX: QUESTIONNAIRE   206

INDEX   217

Worksheet List

Worksheet 2.1	Short obsessive compulsive scale (SOCS)	26
Worksheet 5.1	Understanding my obsessions and compulsions	47
Worksheet 5.2	Understanding my OCD trap	52
Worksheet 5.3:	Understanding my child's obsessions and compulsions	56
Worksheet 7.1	How anxiety affects me	71
Worksheet 8.1	My OCD diary	82
Worksheet 8.2	Making my OCD ladder	86
Worksheet 8.3	Making an action plan	90
Worksheet 9.1	How to break my OCD rules	97
Worksheet 9.2	My exposure and response prevention (E/RP) exercise	101
Worksheet 9.3	Updating my OCD ladder	104
Worksheet 9.4	What progress have I made?	106
Worksheet 10.1	My anxiety graphs	112
Worksheet 11.1	Making an OCD timetable	122
Worksheet 11.2	How to understand difficulties with E/RP exercises	128
Worksheet 12.1	How to understand my thoughts	135

Worksheet 12.2   Having helpful thoughts   138
Worksheet 12.3   Thinking more helpful OCD thoughts   143
Worksheet 13.1   How to put my thoughts on trial   150
Worksheet 13.2   How to make my own responsibility pie-chart   155
Worksheet 14.1   My behavioural experiment   162
Worksheet 14.2   How to make sense of my behavioural experiment   169
Worksheet 15.1   An action plan for the future – Part I   175
Worksheet 15.2   An action plan for the future – Part II   180

List of Figures

Figure 1   Examples of obsessions and compulsions   23
Figure 2   How speaking to Sasha could lead to worry   41
Figure 3   Thinking differently about speaking to Sasha   42
Figure 4   The OCD trap   48
Figure 5   Jake's OCD trap   51
Figure 6   Caught in the OCD trap: anxiety remains   76
Figure 7   Fighting OCD: anxiety reduces with practice at resisting
              compulsions   76
Figure 8   Sam's OCD diary   83
Figure 9   Oliver's OCD ladder   88
Figure 10   Lisa's small OCD exposure steps   99
Figure 11   Lucia's exposure and response prevention exercise   102
Figure 12   Jayne's 'thoughts on trial' chart   149
Figure 13   Justin's responsibility pie-chart ratings   153
Figure 14   Justin's pie-chart   154
Figure 15   Ashley's first behavioural experiment result   165
Figure 16   Ashley's second behavioural experiment result   167

Part A

UNDERSTANDING YOUR OCD

In this first part of the book we are going to get a better understanding of a problem called 'obsessive compulsive disorder', or OCD. You will find out how to recognize whether you have OCD and what it means for you. You will also learn more about the symptoms of OCD. You can read about how to get help from your doctor, and also find out about the treatments that work best. The recommended treatment (called 'cognitive behaviour therapy', or CBT) is explained in detail so that you can begin to get an idea of how treatment works.

Chapter 1   **About this Book**

WHY SHOULD I READ THIS BOOK?

You are likely to be looking at this book if you think you have a problem called 'obsessive compulsive disorder', or OCD.

- You may be wondering if you have OCD.

- You might be pretty sure you have OCD.

- You might have been told you have OCD by a doctor.

Someone might have got this book for you, or you might have found it yourself. You may be reluctant to look at it, or think that it will be really boring, or unhelpful. Well...if you have got this far it will be worthwhile having at least a quick look!

This book is for young people who have got OCD. It has been written to help you understand OCD better, and to help you recover.

OCD can be an annoying, upsetting illness, and at its worst it can get in the way of your life. This book does two main things:

1. It explains what OCD is. It explains how OCD works to make you feel so stuck, and why it can make you unhappy. To get better from OCD you need to really understand it: KNOWLEDGE IS POWER!

2. It teaches you how to fight OCD. It will show you ways of fighting OCD that really work.

You do not need to read this book all at once. You might want to read the first few chapters to get information and then think about how you want to use the rest of the book. One of the best ways to use it if you have OCD, is to work through it chapter by chapter, with a helper such as a parent. As you will see, each chapter has a section called 'Advice for parents or carers'; this will help them to support you in overcoming OCD. You can read those sections too, or you may prefer to skip past them.

As you work through the book you will find that you get more and more powerful at understanding OCD and learning strategies for fighting it.

HOW SHOULD I USE THIS BOOK?

Here are suggestions on how to use this book, depending on how bad your OCD is.

I am wondering if I have OCD

You might have noticed that you are feeling a bit worried. Maybe you have noticed some unpleasant thoughts, and annoying habits?

If so, this book will help you work out if you have OCD. There are checklists and questionnaires to complete to help you decide. If you think that you might have OCD, the first step is to tell an adult you trust about your worries. He or she might suggest that you go to see your doctor. You might have a problem that is *not* OCD or you might not have a problem at all!

I think that I have a few OCD symptoms, like unpleasant thoughts that keep coming into my mind, and annoying habits or rituals

These could be the symptoms of mild OCD. You should see your doctor who will work this out with you. Your doctor may suggest that you are referred on to a mental health professional. This book will also help you to recover. You can use this book to learn ways to stop these unpleasant thoughts and habits, and stop your problems getting any worse. You can use it with a helper, who might be a parent or another adult you trust. You could also use it if you are waiting for help from your doctor or another health professional.

I definitely have OCD symptoms, and they are starting to get in the way of my life

Your unpleasant thoughts and rituals are likely to be distressing, taking up a lot of time and maybe preventing you from doing many of the things you like doing. You will need to talk this though with your doctor who will arrange for you to see someone who knows about treating OCD in young people. You should be offered cognitive behaviour therapy (more about that later) and possibly medication. You might want to use this book while you are waiting for treatment, and alongside the treatment you get from a mental health professional.

My OCD symptoms are so upsetting that they are interfering with my life a great deal, I find it difficult to do many things I used to enjoy, and sometimes I can't get to school or leave the house

It sounds like your OCD has really taken a hold on you and is severely disrupting your life. You can still use this book to help yourself start to recover from OCD, especially alongside any other help that you are receiving. You will probably also need to see a mental health professional for treatment. You might need a combination of cognitive behaviour therapy and medication, and you might need to be seen by a specialist in OCD if you are not getting better. This might be in a child and family centre, specialist clinic or hospital.

WHAT ARE THE TREATMENTS FOR OCD?

We know that there are two sorts of treatment that work to help people with OCD. These are:

- a *talking* treatment called cognitive behaviour therapy (or CBT)

- specific sorts of *medication* called serotonin re-uptake inhibitors (or SRIs).

We know that these treatments work because they have been tried in lots of children, young people and adults with OCD. Doctors and scientists have carried out research (clinical trials) to show that these treatments are effective and that they do not have serious risks. You will find out more about these treatments in Chapters 3 and 4 of the book. After looking at all the research on OCD, experts in the UK have developed national guidelines that describe how to diagnose and treat it. There are very similar guidelines in the USA and other countries. The people who help you with your OCD should know about these guidelines and follow them. This book is based on these guidelines and on the principles of cognitive behaviour therapy. The next chapter will help *you* to understand more about OCD.

SUMMARY

- Reading this book will help you become an expert in OCD. Becoming an expert is the first step towards your recovery.

- There are treatments that work to make OCD better. These are:

    ○ cognitive behaviour therapy

    ○ medication

- There are national guidelines that describe how to diagnose and treat OCD.

- Working through this book is likely to help you get better as it will teach you how to fight OCD using the principles of cognitive behaviour therapy.

Now turn to the next chapter on page 19

ADVICE FOR PARENTS OR CARERS

RECOMMENDED TREATMENTS

In the UK, the health service has guidelines for good health care, which are produced by a government body called the National Institute for Health and Clinical Excellence (NICE). There are NICE guidelines on how to assess and treat people with OCD. If you go to your doctor or another clinician such as a psychologist or psychiatrist for help with OCD, they should be following these NICE guidelines. Although other countries may not have official national guidelines, people treating OCD internationally are in agreement about which treatments to recommend. In this book we make suggestions that are in line with recommendations from NICE.

It is recognized that people will have OCD of different severities. In some people it may be very mild and not get in the way of their life very much, but in others it may have been around for a long time and might have become very troublesome.

It is recommended that ideally all young people with OCD should be offered the opportunity to try cognitive behaviour therapy (CBT). It may not suit everyone, and sometimes it is difficult to find a qualified cognitive behaviour therapist near to where you live. Some children with OCD will also benefit from treatment with medication, and this should be available too.

This book describes the principles of cognitive behaviour therapy as recommended by experts treating children and young people with OCD. We recommend that the young person works through the material with an adult (whether parent or professional) to get the best out of this book.

- It will not necessarily replace the need for a young person to work with a cognitive behaviour therapist, but it teaches the same strategies that therapists will use.

- Some therapists and children might want to use this book together.

- Some children might want to use this book with their parents or another helper while they are waiting for therapy.

For some children with very mild OCD, or OCD that has only been present for a short time, using this book with a helper might help them recover completely. However, we do not know this for certain, and there have not been research studies to prove this. So for the time being, we would recommend that everyone with OCD be assessed by, and offered treatment from, an experienced professional.

What is OCD?

This chapter will help you to understand more about obsessive compulsive disorder (OCD). By the end of this chapter you should have a better idea of whether or not you have OCD and how it might be affecting you. By increasing your knowledge about OCD you will be better prepared to fight it.

SO WHAT IS OCD?

To help you to understand more about OCD we have included some stories of other young people. However, it is important to remember that symptoms of OCD can be different for different people, so your OCD may be similar to, or completely different from the examples that we describe. The two stories below outline Claire and Liam's OCD symptoms.

CLAIRE

Claire, aged 13, had unwanted thoughts about her friends and family being hurt. These thoughts frightened her and made her feel guilty and confused. Whenever Claire had a thought about something awful happening to someone she loved she would imagine a good thing happening to them instead. For example, if a picture of her mum in a car crash popped into her head she would try to imagine her smiling and laughing with her friends. Claire also spent time arranging her books and pencil case when she experienced an unpleasant thought as this helped her feel in control. Both of these behaviours made her feel that she had prevented her awful thoughts from coming true. Claire sometimes felt embarrassed as she knew that her behaviour did not make sense, but it was the only way that she felt able to reduce her feelings of guilt and worry. However, the behaviour only worked to reduce her guilt and worry for a short while, until the next thought came along.

LIAM

Liam, aged 15, checked the locks of doors and windows up to twenty times a day. He was careful to do everything in a particular order – pushing in the latch with all his force and then tapping the lock ten times. He became very upset if he was interrupted, as it meant that he would have to start his checking rituals all over again. Sometimes it would take Liam up to two hours to complete this routine and it made him very angry with himself. Liam found it difficult to leave the house, always doubting that he had completed the checking ritual perfectly and that it was safe to leave. He hated anyone leaving the house after him and he would phone his parents many times throughout the day to ask whether or not they had locked everything properly. He would become so frustrated with himself that he would cry but he just did not know how to stop!

Although their stories are different, Claire and Liam both have obsessive compulsive disorder. We know this because they both have unpleasant

thoughts that keep coming back and are difficult to stop. We call these types of thoughts *obsessions*. Claire and Liam also carry out certain behaviours over and over again. Their behaviours do not make sense, yet they feel they must carry them out. We call these types of behaviours *compulsions*. This is where the name 'obsessive compulsive disorder' comes from. Often compulsions are carried out to reduce or cancel out an obsession.

As well as carrying out particular behaviours (like checking or ordering), OCD can make you want to avoid particular situations or things that might trigger an obsession. Liam, for example, began to avoid leaving the house as this meant that he had fewer worrying thoughts about his house.

When someone has obsessions and compulsions that:

- disrupt their life

- cause them distress, and

- occupy their time for more than an hour each day

they are said to have obsessive compulsive disorder.

Claire's obsessions include unwanted thoughts and images about bad things happening to the people she cares about, while Liam's obsession is his repeated thought that his house is not safe. Claire's compulsions include cancelling out her thoughts by imagining good things happening and by arranging her belongings. Liam's compulsions include checking, ordering and repeating when he locks doors and windows. Their obsessions make them anxious, and their compulsions help reduce this anxiety, but only until the thought comes into their mind again. Claire and Liam are caught in a trap of OCD. This is explained in more detail in Chapter 5, 'Understanding My OCD'.

THE VARIOUS SYMPTOMS OF OCD

When OCD is discussed in newspapers and on television, we often hear about washing and checking compulsions, and about obsessions that concern dirt and germs. However, there are all sorts of obsessions and compulsions that a person can suffer with. Some are more common than others but no two people's symptoms are exactly the same.

Many people do not realize that they have OCD as they have never heard of their symptoms before. Some people feel like they are the only one with this sort of problem. Even if your particular thoughts and behaviours are not mentioned in this book you may still have OCD. It is important to remember the definition of obsessions and compulsions, since how they are experienced (unwanted, distressing) is more important than the type of symptom (e.g. checking, washing). If you have noticed yourself performing behaviours to reduce your worries, and hese behaviours upset you and do not seem to make sense, then they may well be compulsions. Figure 1 illustrates some of the most common obsessions and compulsions.

If you think that you may be suffering from OCD it is important to remember that you are not alone. In fact, up to 2 in every 100 people have suffered with OCD at some point in their life. This means that in a school of 300 students there could be between 3 and 6 people with OCD! Anyone can suffer from OCD and it affects people from all around the world. Some famous people have spoken about their OCD. Maybe you can think of a few?

SOME INFORMATION ABOUT YOUR THOUGHTS

Many people with OCD feel embarrassed or ashamed about their symptoms. Some people worry that they are going mad. It is normal to

Obsessions	Compulsions
• Worries about dirt or germs	• Checking things over and over again
• Worrying about bad things happening	• Squaring things up, or arranging things so that they are 'just right'
• Thinking about doing something wrong	• Counting, repeating and re-doing things
• Worrying about hurting other people or about you being hurt	• Touching, tapping or rubbing things
• Feeling as if you must say, do or remember something	• Washing and cleaning
• Wanting things to be in a particular order	• Asking questions and asking for reassurance
• Having magical thoughts or superstitions	• Collecting and keeping lots of things that you don't need
• Worrying about offending God	• Re-reading or re-writing things
• Unwanted sexual thoughts	

Figure 1 Examples of obsessions and compulsions

KAMAL

Kamal felt urges to count things and add things up. For example, he would always count how many cars passed him on the way to school or how many hours he had slept that week. Whenever he tried to ignore these urges to count, he felt uncomfortable and worried but was unsure why – he just seemed to have a feeling that things were 'not right'. These rituals were beginning to take up so much time that they were distracting him from his school work and his grades were dropping. Although Kamal had heard about OCD he did not think that this was his problem as he had never heard of anyone having symptoms like his before. Having spoken to his doctor, he found out that OCD could affect people in all sorts of different ways, and that his urges were in fact obsessions, and his counting and adding up were compulsions.

have an unwanted thought pop into your mind, but these thoughts tend to upset you more if you have OCD. Unwanted thoughts that pop into someone's head are called *intrusive thoughts*, and it may surprise you to hear that as many as 90 per cent of people have unwanted, intrusive thoughts.

If you ask friends and family they may well tell you that they occasionally have unwanted thoughts that they would never act upon, such as suddenly standing up or shouting out in the middle of an assembly, or imagining themselves falling down the stairs, or having a picture in their head of something awful happening to someone they love. Most people are able to dismiss these thoughts as 'just a thought' and forget about them. People with OCD find this more difficult.

Some people with OCD worry that their intrusive thoughts mean they are a bad person. Claire, for example, worried that she was bad because she pictured violent things happening to her family. However, OCD cannot make you a bad person. Obsessional thoughts have been described as 'hiccups of the brain', because they happen even though we do not want them to. Having them does not mean that you have done anything wrong. In fact we often find that people have obsessions about the things that distress, worry or disgust them most, which is why OCD can seem like such a horrible problem.

Some people worry that thinking their thoughts or talking about them will make them come true. Although you may *feel* as if having these thoughts means they will come true, you probably know that it is impossible to cause or prevent an event just by thinking about it. You can test this out yourself by deliberately trying to make something happen with your thoughts. For example, try to make someone eat something they really don't like just by thinking of them doing it, or try to make your family win the lottery just by thinking that they will. I'm sure this exercise will have shown you that thinking things doesn't make them happen!

DO I HAVE OCD?

There are questionnaires that can help you to think about whether or not you have OCD. Complete the short questionnaire in Worksheet 2.1 on the next page to help you decide if you might have OCD.

You can calculate your total score by adding up your scores for all seven questions. If you score 6 or more this might mean you have OCD, so you should talk to someone you trust about this. However, even with a score of less than 6 you *might* still have OCD. And a score of 6 or above might happen if you have some other problem or worries. *So questionnaires never take the place of getting help, but they can be useful for guidance.*

To be certain about whether or not you have OCD, we would recommend that you be assessed by a professional who knows about this problem. You can read more about this in Chapter 3, 'Can I Get Better from OCD?'.

Worksheet 2.1

Short obsessive compulsive scale (SOCS)*

For each question, put a circle around your answer.

Question	Score 0	Score 1	Score 2
Does your mind often make you do things (such as checking or touching things or counting things) even though you know you don't really have to?	No	A bit	A lot
Are you particularly fussy about keeping your hands clean?	No	A bit	A lot
Do you ever have to do things over and over a certain number of times before they seem quite right?	No	A bit	A lot
Do you ever have trouble finishing your school work or chores because you have to do something over and over again?	No	A bit	A lot
Do you worry a lot if you've done something not exactly the way you like?	No	A bit	A lot

If you have answered 'A lot' to *any* of these questions, please answer the next two questions as well.

	Score 0	Score 1	Score 2
Do these things interfere with your life?	No	A bit	A lot
Do you try to stop them?	No	A bit	A lot

You can calculate your total score by adding up your scores for all seven questions: ('No' = 0; 'A bit' = 1; 'A lot' = 2).

*   See: Uher, R., Heyman, I., Mortimore, C., Frampton, I. and Goodman, R. (2007) 'Screening young people for obsessive compulsive disorder.' *British Journal of Psychiatry 191*, 353–4.

SUMMARY

- Obsessions are unwanted thoughts, pictures or urges that come into your mind. They are unpleasant and repetitive (i.e. they come over and over again) and they may make you feel out of control. Obsessions are usually associated with feelings such as anxiety, disgust and doubt.

- Compulsions are behaviours or actions that are carried out in response to an obsession. You might feel you have to do them over and over again, even if you don't want to or if you know that they don't make sense. Compulsions might be behaviours that other people can see (e.g. washing your hands, checking things) or they might be things you do inside your head that others can't see (e.g. counting, saying something to yourself over and over again).

- Compulsions might initially make you feel less anxious or worried, or they might make an obsession go away, but this is only temporary. Compulsions actually make obsessions stronger and more frequent.

- When obsessions and compulsions make you upset and angry or take up a lot of your time, this is known as obsessive compulsive disorder.

REMEMBER

- OCD is not your fault.
- It does not make you mad or bad.
- OCD affects up to 2 per cent of the population.
- Anyone can suffer from OCD.
- Most people experience unwanted or intrusive thoughts at some time.

Now turn to the next chapter on page 31

ADVICE FOR PARENTS OR CARERS

Reading this section will help you to recognize and understand OCD. The first question you may be wishing to answer is whether or not your child has OCD. Perhaps you have found yourself bewildered by your child's repetitive actions, prolonged behaviours or avoidance of situations. Or maybe you have noticed their intense and frequent worries which persist despite repeated reassurance. You may well have experienced your own distress at these events and made changes in your life to accommodate and manage their worries and behaviours. This section will help you to answer your questions by exploring the basics of OCD, and it helps you learn how to receive a diagnosis and support.

WHAT IS OBSESSIVE COMPULSIVE DISORDER?

OCD is characterized by intrusive, recurring and unpleasant thoughts (obsessions) and repetitive, frustrating and irrational behaviours (compulsions). The behaviours can be physical actions (e.g. tapping, checking, rewriting, washing), or mental rituals (e.g. visualizing a good image to cancel out a bad image). They function to temporarily relieve the stress and distress associated with an obsession. Obsessions and compulsions are often accompanied by feelings of anxiety, guilt, disgust and shame.

Between the ages of 2–6 years, many children have rituals, such as insisting on certain clothes or food, or arranging toys in a particular way. This is part of normal childhood development and enables children to begin to make sense of their world. Similarly, many adults have some ritualized behaviours; consider for example the person who returns to check that their car is locked, or the sports person who likes to wear their 'lucky shirt' for a match. However this is not OCD. Obsessions and compulsions become a disorder when they significantly interfere with a person's life. The behaviours will appear extreme and cause anxiety, anger and upset if they are interrupted or prevented. People with OCD may try to ignore their thoughts but are generally unable to do so because of their overwhelming feelings. The embarrassment or irritation at having to perform lengthy rituals, and the fear of obsessions, may also cause the sufferer to avoid people, activities or places.

OCD can affect people of all ages. Often when adults are diagnosed with OCD, it becomes apparent that they have had the problem since childhood, but they did not get help. This may have been because less was known and understood about the condition and its treatment. We now know that there are some very effective treatments for OCD and that the more quickly a person is treated the better they will do in later life. Recent studies show that OCD may affect 1–2 per cent of the population, which means that it is likely that there are other children in your child's school who will be suffering with it too.

If your child has OCD they may be very embarrassed, ashamed or frightened of their symptoms and find them difficult to talk about. The behaviours that appear senseless and irritating to you, may to them feel like the difference between life and death! You may have noticed their rituals but you may not be sure whether your child has obsessions or what their obsessions might be. This could be because your child finds it difficult to understand or talk about their thoughts, or it may be because the obsessions are not thoughts but are urges or feelings of discomfort that they just cannot tolerate. Alternatively, they may fear that talking about their obsessions will cause them to come true.

Children often feel particularly ashamed if their obsessions are sexual or violent. It is important for you and your child to remember that obsessions are just unwanted thoughts, nothing else. They do not mean anything about your child. In fact obsessions will often involve the things that frighten or embarrass them most.

Many people with OCD worry that they are going 'crazy'. If a young person has OCD, it does not mean that he or she is going crazy. They are normal, but they do have a problem with anxiety and worry. The majority of people with OCD are aware that their worries and concerns are unreasonable and irrational and would rather be free of them. It can be helpful to remind your child that their thoughts and symptoms do not make them mad or dangerous and that they are not alone in their difficulties. Finally, making them aware that they are free to choose to discuss their worries if they wish and helping them to understand that OCD is a very treatable problem, can provide them with the reassurance and motivation they need to begin fighting their difficulties.

DOES MY CHILD HAVE OCD?

To determine whether or not your child has OCD it is important to consider whether or not their thoughts and behaviours:

- cause them upset

- take up too much time (more than an hour a day)

- interfere with their everyday life (e.g. make them late, affect their relationships, cause them to avoid situations, affect their ability to do school work).

There are questionnaires and checklists that can help you and your child think about whether they have OCD. A short questionnaire (Worksheet 2.1) can be found on page 26 of this book. This will give you an indication of whether you need to be concerned about OCD. However, to be certain about a diagnosis you and your child would need to meet with a trained professional. Involving an experienced professional will also help you to think about whether medication or further support might be required at any point while you progress through this book. Your family doctor should be able to help you find the right people to assess and diagnose OCD and provide further support if necessary. You can read more about this in Chapter 3 of the book.

WHY DOES MY CHILD HAVE OCD?

If your child is suffering with OCD you may be asking yourself why. Many parents worry that they might be in some way to blame for their child's OCD but it is very important to remember that OCD is not your fault and neither is it the fault of your child. There is no simple explanation as to why one person develops OCD and why another does not, but there are some known risk factors that may make some people more vulnerable to developing the condition than others. If you are wanting to find out more about the risk factors associated with OCD, then there are additional reading materials and information websites provided in the resource list at the end of this book. However, it is very difficult to be certain about the exact causes of an individual's OCD, and it is not necessary that you understand the cause of your child's OCD in order to help them overcome the condition.

Chapter 3

Can I Get Better from OCD?

If you have got OCD or are worried that you might have OCD, it means that some unpleasant and time-consuming things are happening to you. The main symptoms of OCD – the unwanted, distressing thoughts (obsessions) and the upsetting, distressing rituals (compulsions) – are getting in the way of your life.

There are several important things to realize right away, that you might have read about in the previous chapters:

- OCD is a recognized illness and there are good treatments that really work.

- You are not on your own: OCD occurs in up to 2 young people in every 100.

- You are not crazy or weird!

HOW TO GET HELP

Don't avoid asking for help! People have all sorts of reasons for putting off telling someone about their problems or asking for help. You might feel silly or embarrassed, you might feel you should be able to cope on your own, or you may worry that by talking about your thoughts the problem will get worse.

HARDEEP

This is what Hardeep wrote about feeling silly when she first tried to explain her OCD.

'One of the hardest things about starting treatment was having to talk about what was happening to me. I'd only just found out that it was an illness called OCD that other people had too and I still felt really silly. I didn't want to discuss my habits with anyone at first. It just sounded so stupid when I tried to explain how OCD makes me check the light switch so many times, even though I know it's definitely off. In the end though, it was such a relief to meet other people who knew what I was talking about. Don't let OCD force you into keeping it a secret; telling other people you trust is the first step to fighting back.'

So don't keep OCD a secret. Telling someone you can trust about OCD is a good way to start fighting back. You could talk to a parent, a family friend, teacher or school nurse. Remember: OCD likes to keep things secret, which helps it to stay in charge!

There are people outside your friends and family who know about OCD and can help you. Usually the first person to see is your doctor. It might help to remember that doctors are used to hearing about all sorts of problems. Below are some tips to help you speak to your doctor.

- Take someone with you if you can, if this would be easier.

- Take some written notes describing your symptoms if you think you might find it tricky to explain.

- It might help to describe how much time your obsessions and compulsions take up and whether they stop you from doing anything.

- Maybe take a copy of the questionnaire that you completed in Chapter 2.

- Say that you think you might have OCD.

The doctor might suggest you see a clinical psychologist, a child psychiatrist, or another sort of mental health worker who understands young people.

What is a clinical psychologist?

Child clinical psychologists are experienced in helping young people with thoughts, feelings and behaviours. Clinical psychologists are trained in cognitive behavioural therapy.

What is a psychiatrist?

Child psychiatrists are medical doctors who have additional training in children's mental health. Psychiatrists can prescribe medication and also help with cognitive behaviour therapy.

What is a cognitive behaviour therapist?

Cognitive behaviour therapists can come from a variety of professions (nursing, psychology, psychiatry, social work) and may have additional training in cognitive behaviour therapy.

MARIE

Marie wrote about how it made her feel better when she went to her first appointment, but how scared she had felt before.

'The most helpful thing I heard at my first appointment was the reassurance that I was not going mad. I'd been struggling with all these crazy thoughts for so long and was terrified that unless I did certain things something terrible was going to happen to my Mum. I was sure I was having a breakdown or something, so it was really scary going along to the clinic for the first time – I thought they might lock me up. It was so reassuring when the doctor explained how OCD works, and that it's a well-known illness, and that there are good treatments. With cognitive behaviour therapy and sometimes medication, you can get things back under control.'

WHAT ARE THE TREATMENTS FOR OCD?

For everyone with OCD the first part of treatment is getting information and really understanding the problem.

- Everyone with OCD should be offered a talking treatment called *cognitive behaviour therapy*. This is called CBT for short, and we'll find out more about it in Chapter 4, 'What is Cognitive Behaviour Therapy?'.

- Some people with OCD will benefit from specific *medication*, and this should be discussed with you.

HOW DO WE KNOW TREATMENTS WORK?

Not all treatments work for all sorts of problems. However, we know that CBT and specific medications work for OCD because they have been studied scientifically in lots of people with OCD.

There are many other treatments around that are offered to people who have problems with emotions and behaviour. These do not work for

OCD. If you have another problem as well as OCD, such as depression, your therapist might suggest that you have another treatment as well. But you should still get the effective OCD treatments.

Treatments that have not been found to work on their own for OCD include:

- family therapy (although CBT can sometimes involve the whole family)
- counselling
- other sorts of psychotherapy such as psychoanalysis
- hypnosis
- relaxation
- acupuncture
- herbal remedies
- medications that are not serotonin medications (SRIs or SSRIs).

SUMMARY

- Don't keep OCD a secret: tell someone you trust so you can get help.
- OCD is a treatable problem.
- Go to see your doctor if you think you might have OCD.
- The first step in treatment is having a good assessment to make sure the problem is OCD and everyone understands about it.
- The first step in recovery is learning more about OCD.
- The effective treatments are cognitive behaviour therapy (CBT) and medication.
- You should be offered CBT first.
- Some people may also need medication.

Now turn to the next chapter on page 40

ADVICE FOR PARENTS OR CARERS

GETTING HELP FOR YOUR CHILD WITH OCD

You may have noticed a change in your child's emotions or behaviour, or they may have come to you saying that they have some worries. If you and your child think that OCD might be the problem, use this approach:

- Gently encourage them to explain to you what they are experiencing.

- Don't put too much pressure on them to talk, but just make it clear that you are interested and available.

- Find out a bit about OCD yourself, so you are not surprised by the sorts of symptoms your child might be having.

Don't forget that not all worries and repetitive behaviours are OCD. Children can have these symptoms for a wide range of reasons. It might be completely normal and they will out grow it. On the other hand, it might be another sort of problem – so you should still see your doctor to get some advice.

WHAT IF MY CHILD DOES NOT WANT HELP?

Your child may need some gentle encouragement to see your doctor. They might be helped by reading the section above in this book, and looking at the website www.ocdyouth.info.

If your child is at a stage where they are distressed but do not want help, it can be very difficult and upsetting to watch them struggle. If you feel that you need any support yourself in this process you may wish to discuss your situation with your doctor, look at OCD websites or call one of the support lines detailed at the back of this book.

WHAT ASSESSMENT WILL THE DOCTOR DO, AND WHAT TREATMENTS WILL BE RECOMMENDED?

Your doctor may know a lot about OCD and will help work out whether your child does have OCD. In the UK, the National Institute for Health and Clinical Excellence (NICE) has recently issued guidelines on the treatment of OCD. UK doctors should be aware of the NICE guidelines. Other countries also have guidelines for assessing and treating OCD. It is possible to access these guidelines on the NICE website (www.nice.org.uk) – look out for the version for people with OCD and their families.

Diagnosing OCD may involve your doctor asking your child direct questions about obsessions and compulsions. If your doctor does think your child has OCD, they are likely to refer on to a child mental health professional who will carry out a more detailed assessment and start some treatment.

Some doctors may have a child mental health worker linked with their practice. This person should know the symptoms of OCD and be able to work out with you and your child whether OCD is the main problem. They should also screen for other common problems that can be confused with OCD or may occur with it. These include:

- ordinary childhood worries

- other anxiety problems such as generalized anxiety

- phobias

- depression

- developmental problems such as autism spectrum disorders

- Tourette syndrome.

As part of the assessment they may use a structured interview for OCD. If your child does have OCD the two effective treatments should be discussed with you, and your child should be offered cognitive behaviour therapy (CBT). Depending on how severe the OCD is, what other problems there may be, and what you and your child want, the CBT could be offered in different ways. For example, you might be offered one, or a combination, of these options:

- If the OCD is very mild, you and your child, with the help of a therapist, could use a self-help book such as this one.

- You and your child could see a cognitive behaviour therapist for a series of sessions. You will learn a technique called 'exposure and response prevention' to teach you how to fight the OCD.

- If the OCD is more severe or more complicated you may be referred to the next level of child mental health services, where you should also be offered CBT.

- Occasionally a doctor (child psychiatrist) might suggest that your child tries some medication as well as having CBT, if they think this will help recovery.

BUT remember: whatever kind of mental health specialist you see (nurse, psychologist, doctor or other) the main treatment they should be offering you is CBT. You should feel confident that they are trained in this sort of therapy, so don't be shy about asking about this.

USEFUL FACTS: MEDICATION

Specific medications can be helpful in OCD. This has been shown in several clinical trials in young people, and the results from all of these studies are clearly summarized in the UK NICE guidance. The medications that work all act on a brain chemical called serotonin. The medications most likely to be recommended for your child are the selective serotonin re-uptake inhibitors (SSRIs). These include sertraline, fluoxetine, fluvoxamine, citalopram and paroxetine. Sometimes the medication clomipramine is recommended which also acts on serotonin. Your doctor will explain any possible side-effects, but in general these medications are well tolerated. If side-effects do occur these usually occur in the first few days. If the first medicine tried doesn't help or produces side-effects, another can be tried. The most common side-effects are feeling a bit less hungry, or having a slight headache. Sometimes young people taking SSRIs feel more anxious for a few days, or even get distressing thoughts about harming themselves. This is very rare, and usually goes away, but the person prescribing needs to be told if this happens, and consideration given whether to change or stop the medication.

If medication is going to help, you usually begin to see a response after 2–3 weeks, and rarely before this. Usually the young person will be given a low dose to start with, and the dose will be gradually increased. Sometimes it is necessary to use high doses of SSRIs to successfully treat OCD, and it may be suggested that your son or daughter tries to increase the dose to the highest they can tolerate without side-effects. In some cases of severe OCD, that has not responded to two or more different SSRIs, it is suggested that a low dose of a different medication is added. These are medicines that act on a different brain chemical, dopamine. These are added to the SSRI in a very small dose, and you will be warned of side-effects such as sleepiness or weight gain.

If medication has been helpful to your child in their recovery, it is usually suggested that they stay on the SSRI medication for at least 6–12 months once they are well again. This is to consolidate recovery, and minimize the chances of relapse. It is strongly recommended that, if at all possible, everyone with OCD has CBT even if they have medication as well. This may minimize the chances of relapsing when the time comes to stop medication. Sometimes it is helpful to have a couple of 'top-up' CBT sessions as your child comes off medication.

Chapter 4

What is Cognitive Behaviour Therapy?

By now you will have read that cognitive behaviour therapy (or CBT) is the main type of treatment to help you overcome your OCD. CBT is a type of talking treatment, and it's the only type of talking treatment that's been shown to be helpful in overcoming OCD (although instead of talking with you face-to-face, we'll be talking with you through the book). The sorts of things that we'll be introducing you to in this book are the same sorts of things that a doctor would talk to you about if you went to see them in a clinic.

CBT is based on the idea that how we feel is influenced by how we think and how we behave. Let's use the following simple example to illustrate this Figure 2.

You can see from this that we're likely to feel worried about speaking to Sasha because we haven't done something that we had promised to do. But, we could have felt very differently about this situation if we had thought and done something different. See Figure 3 for an example.

Although the situation is the same, our feelings about the situation can be very different if we choose to think and do things differently. The good news is that *we can learn* how to use our thoughts and behaviour (i.e. how to think and do things differently) in order to feel differently about things. Although this is a very simple example, that's essentially what CBT is all about. It's about learning to use your thoughts and behaviour to help you feel better about things that you might feel upset or worried about.

SITUATION
Remembering that we haven't telephoned Sasha, although we promised to call her yesterday.

↓

THOUGHTS
Oh no, I promised to call Sasha and I haven't. She'll think I'm awful!

↓

BEHAVIOUR
Put off calling her.

↓

FEELINGS
Worried/anxious.

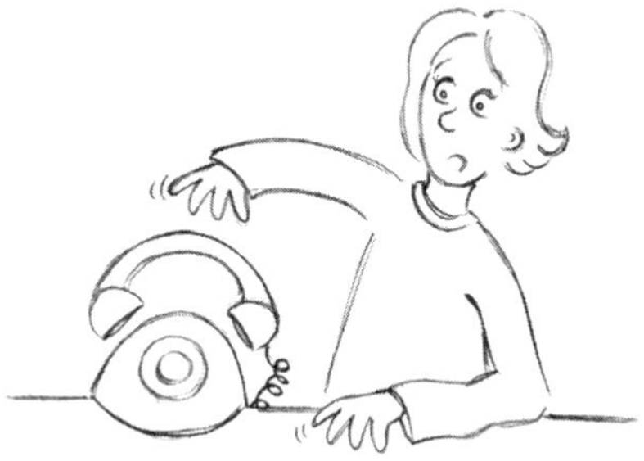

Figure 2 How speaking to Sasha could lead to worry

COGNITIVE BEHAVIOUR THERAPY (CBT) FOR OCD

You will know already that OCD can take control of your thoughts and actions, and can make you feel very anxious, worried or upset. CBT can help to overcome OCD by helping you to learn new ways of thinking and doing things in response to the obsessions that you get. Learning how to do this will help you to feel less anxious, upset or frightened by the OCD thoughts, and will help you to confront the fears and doubts that you may have. This might sound difficult to do, but it is something that many other young people (and adults) with OCD have done and it is possible!

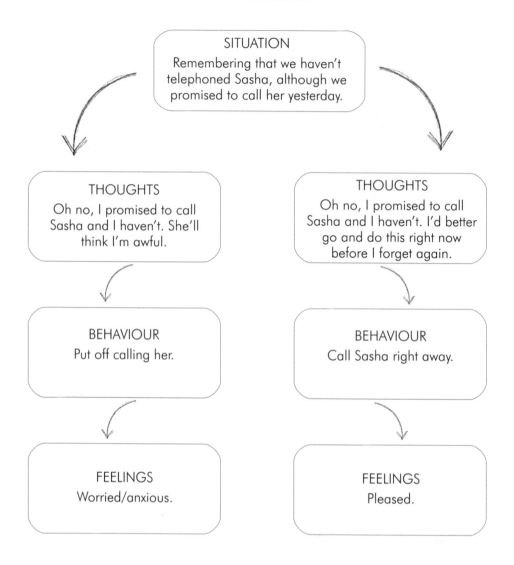

Figure 3 Thinking differently about speaking to Sasha

We will be taking things one step at a time, and will teach you step-by-step some new skills. The CBT skills and strategies that you learn will help you to fight back against the OCD little-by-little, and to gradually win back control of your own thoughts and behaviours.

As with learning anything new, some things might feel a little awkward or difficult at first. The more you practise them, the easier they will become. Each of the chapters in Part B of this book will introduce you to a new skill or strategy that you might find helpful in overcoming your OCD.

SOME FACTS ABOUT CBT FOR OCD

1. Don't expect that you'll overcome your OCD immediately. It will take some time and some practice. If you set aside some time each day to put toward fighting your OCD, you can expect to see some changes within about 6–8 weeks. For some people, it may take a little longer and it may be 10–20 weeks before you see some changes. Hang in there. The more you persist, the easier it will become.

2. CBT isn't a magical cure. Like all things, you will get more out of it if you put more into it. It will take active participation, effort and practice.

3. Not everyone will get the same amount of benefit from CBT. The things that you learn in this book might lead to sudden and dramatic improvements, but it is more likely that slow and steady progress will happen. The changes you are able to make through CBT might be small or large.

4. At the end of working through this book, you may not be rid of all of your OCD symptoms. This is normal. Many young people who complete face-to-face CBT for their OCD will be in the same situation.

5. The benefits you get from CBT are likely to last after you stop using this book. The strategies that you learn will be helpful not just for your OCD, but for other times when you feel anxious or worried.

SUMMARY

- Cognitive behaviour therapy (CBT) will teach you about how thoughts, feelings and behaviour all affect each other.

- The main aim of using CBT strategies in this book will be to help you to fight back against OCD and not carry out your compulsions.

- As you learn to think and do things differently, you will be able to see that the anxiety you feel as a result of OCD will begin to go away.

- As you start to feel less anxious and worried about OCD, you will begin to feel more confident to resist doing what OCD wants you to do and to confront your fears and doubts.

- Using CBT strategies to overcome your OCD will take time, patience and lots of practice. The more you put into it, the more you will get out of it.

Now turn to the next chapter on page 46

ADVICE FOR PARENTS OR CARERS

This section presents a brief overview of cognitive behaviour therapy, or CBT. This is the only psychological therapy that research has shown is helpful in overcoming OCD. Please read through this chapter. Throughout the book, each chapter will provide a section for parents that will help you to consider what you might be able to do to help your child in making the most out of CBT and out of this book. There are several different roles that parents or carers can take, and these are described in more detail in Chapter 6. It will be up to you and your child to discuss together how you can help them in a way that they will find useful and supportive.

Chapter 5

Understanding My OCD

Now that you have a good understanding of what OCD is, it is important that you start to become an expert in your own OCD. Starting to understand how your own OCD works will help you to gain power over it and take back control. This is one of the most important parts of your recovery from OCD.

UNDERSTANDING YOUR OBSESSIONS AND COMPULSIONS

Many people find it difficult to distinguish between their obsessions and compulsions. Use Worksheet 5.1 to think about your own obsessions and compulsions. To help with this, you may find it useful to remind yourself of the differences between obsessions and compulsions:

- *Obsessions* are thoughts, pictures or urges in your mind that are repetitive and feel out of control. They are accompanied by feelings such as anxiety, disgust and doubt.

- *Compulsions* are repetitive actions that are carried out to try to cancel out or neutralize an obsession.

- When obsessions and compulsions make you upset and angry or take up a lot of your time, it is known as *obsessive compulsive disorder*.

Understanding my obsessions and compulsions

Obsessions	Compulsions

THE OCD TRAP

The way that OCD keeps you worrying about upsetting thoughts and doing rituals is often called the OCD trap. When an *obsession* pops into your mind it causes you to worry. The worry is unpleasant and makes you anxious and distressed, which means that you will want to do something to stop it. This leads you to perform a *compulsion*, which temporarily reduces your worry. You feel better in the short term, because your anxiety has subsided. However, when an obsessional thought creeps into your mind again you will need to do more compulsions to feel better. This is how the cycle of obsessions and compulsions begins, and it is called the OCD trap. Have a look at Figure 3 to see how this works.

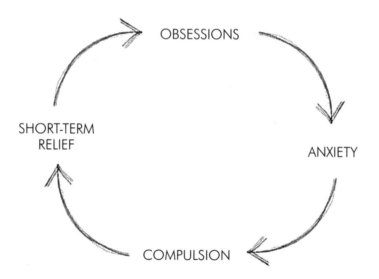

Figure 4 The OCD trap

Like you, young people caught in a trap of OCD find it hard to stop their compulsions for two reasons.

1. Once they have completed their compulsions they feel less worried. However, this only reduces their worry *in the short term*. The next time they think the obsessional thought, they will need to do more compulsions. Unfortunately, over time, OCD demands that you do more and more compulsions to bring the same relief, always leaving you doubtful and uncertain that you have done enough.

2. People with OCD feel that they cannot risk the possibility of what might happen if they did not perform a compulsion. Often they fear that they will not be able to cope with their worry, or even that the worry will never end! Because of this, people with OCD continue to perform compulsions and never allow themselves the opportunity to test their beliefs, or to learn that their worries will fade.

To really illustrate this idea, imagine there is a boy in your school who covers himself in red paint every day before coming to school. You ask the boy why he covers himself in red paint and he replies 'To protect myself from being attacked by lions'. Puzzled, you explain that there are no lions in the school and he answers 'I know, that's because I paint myself in red paint!' The boy never comes to school without his red paint, and so he never has the opportunity to learn that he would not be attacked by lions anyway!

HOW DOES YOUR OCD TRAP WORK?

So what does your OCD trap look like? Before you start to draw out your own OCD trap, take a look at the example of Jake. This will help you understand how OCD works.

JAKE

Jake was terrified of offending people and worried that if he ever did anything wrong he would die. Every day he spent time thinking about whether or not he had upset other people and he would ring them to check and say sorry. Jake spent each day praying for forgiveness, but gradually his prayers had become longer and more complicated. They also had to be completed perfectly and in a particular order. The worries and prayers were preventing him from spending time with his friends. They were making him miserable, but his fear of going to hell made it difficult for him to stop.

What are Jake's obsessions and compulsions?

- Jake's obsessions include a fear of dying and going to hell.

- Jake's compulsions include praying, checking that he hasn't offended others, and apologizing.

- His compulsions reduce the anxiety that results from his fears about dying. But because he always does them, they never allow him the opportunity to test out whether his thoughts will come true, or to learn that his anxiety will fade without a compulsion. His OCD trap is shown in Figure 5.

DRAWING YOUR OWN OCD TRAP

Now that you have a list of your own obsessions and compulsions we can think about how, like for Jake, *they keep you trapped in a cycle of OCD.* Turn to Worksheet 5.2 on page 52, and in the box labelled OBSESSION, insert one of your obsessions from the list. The next box refers to the feelings that you get when you have had this obsession. Your obsessions might make you feel worried, scared or fearful. Anxiety is a good word to describe these feelings. Maybe you have other feelings too, such as frustration, disgust or anger? Use the ANXIETY box to describe how the obsession makes you feel. It is this unpleasant feeling that makes you want to do a compulsion or avoid a situation.

Sometimes people are so used to doing a compulsion after an obsession that they have *forgotten* how their obsessions make them feel. If you have noticed this, imagine how you would feel if you were prevented from doing your compulsive behaviour – and write these feelings down. These are the feelings that keep your OCD trap going even though you may not always be aware of them.

Once you have completed this box think about whether there is a particular compulsion from your list that is connected to this thought. Insert this information into the COMPULSION box. You have probably noticed that your unpleasant feelings following a compulsion disappear for a little while when you have performed a compulsion. The word 'relief' is used to explain this.

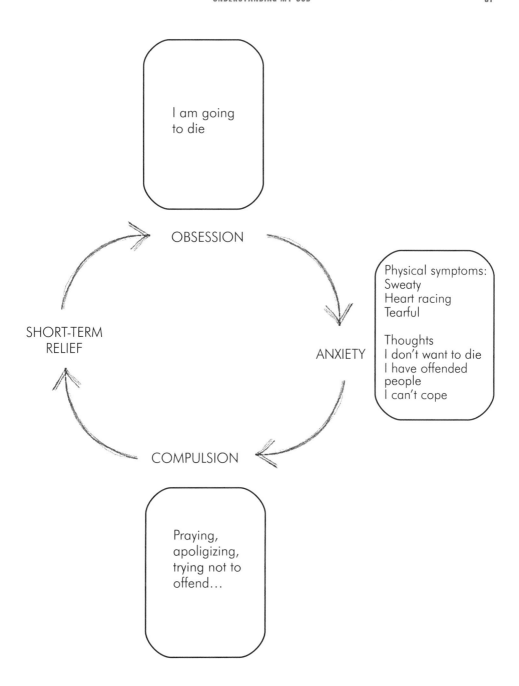

Figure 5 Jake's OCD trap

Understanding my OCD trap

Spend some time thinking about how OCD traps *you*. Fill in the boxes below to help you understand your own OCD trap.

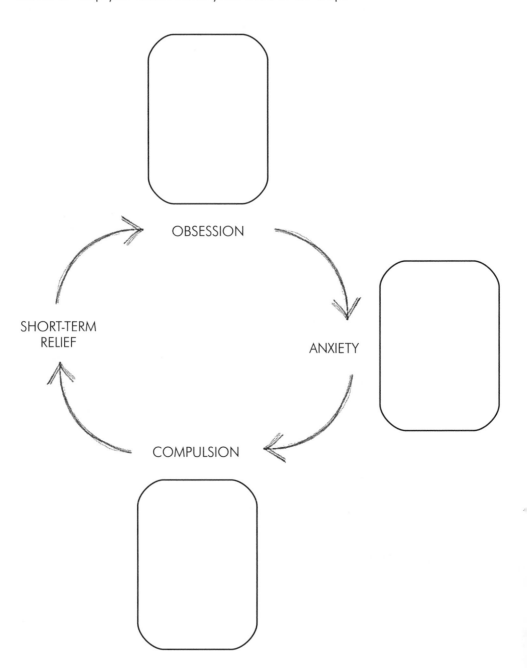

Remember: People caught in the trap of OCD find it hard to stop their compulsions for two reasons:

1. Their compulsions *do* seem to reduce their worry in the short term, which tricks them into thinking they are useful.

2. They feel that they cannot risk the possibility of what might happen if they did not perform a compulsion, and so never have the opportunity to discover that their beliefs won't come true – or to learn that their worries will fade.

WHAT DOES OCD MAKE ME AVOID?

OCD can also cause people to avoid all sorts of situations, places and people that might start up obsessions and make them feel anxious or upset. Jake, for example, began avoiding talking to other people, as he thought that this would prevent him from being rude. Use the space below to list the things that OCD makes *you* avoid.

WHAT WOULD LIFE BE LIKE WITHOUT OCD?

Use the space below to describe the way in which OCD gets in the way of your life. What things in life would be better without OCD?

SUMMARY

- Understanding how OCD traps you is the first step to your recovery.

- You can learn how to break the OCD trap in the next chapter of the book.

- OCD makes you avoid things to feel better, but this only makes you feel better in the short-term.

Now turn to the next part on page 59

ADVICE FOR PARENTS OR CARERS

In this chapter your child has been given the space to think about his or her own obsessions and compulsions, and how these function to keep them caught in what we call 'the OCD trap'. Use this section as your own opportunity to think about your child's OCD and the impact that it has on them and on the family.

YOUR CHILD'S OBSESSIONS AND COMPULSIONS

Often parents have a fair understanding of their child's compulsions as they are likely to have witnessed them first-hand. Mental rituals, however, can be more difficult to spot, although there are some signs that you could watch out for.

During a mental ritual your child may appear *distracted* or *absent*. One parent described their child as 'in a trance'. Before she had heard about mental rituals she was concerned that something more serious than OCD was occurring. However, as her son felt able to gradually open up about his symptoms she realized that he had been involved in an elaborate and complex ritual to cancel out obsessions.

Obsessions are difficult to know about or understand if your child is unable or too distressed to talk about worries. Don't worry if your child feels unable to explain obsessions at the moment. You will still be able to support them in the recovery process.

Use Worksheet 5.3 to list the obsessions and compulsions that you feel affect your child. You can add to these as you learn more about your child's OCD. Once you have completed this list, you could use the information to think about how your child remains stuck in an OCD trap. You may find it helpful to review the main section of this chapter for this. If your child feels able to share their work in this section you could sit down together and compare your results. You could also use this opportunity to check your child's understanding of what they have read and learnt so far.

Understanding my child's obsessions and compulsions

Obsessions	Compulsions

HOW HAS OCD AFFECTED THE FAMILY?

In addition to influencing your child, OCD is likely to have affected you and your family. Any loving parent finds it tough to see their child in distress, and you may have found yourself caught up in their obsessions and compulsions in an effort to lessen their upset.

- Perhaps you have washed clothes and possessions that did not need washing because OCD has caused your child to fear that they are dangerously dirty.

- Perhaps you have provided reassurance to a child whose OCD has caused them to be excessively concerned for your safety.

- You may have allowed your child to stay home from school, or given in to the demands to close the door in a particular way, or even to walk out of the house in a certain order!

The list is endless and it is incredibly rare to speak to a parent who has not been caught in their child's OCD trap. In the short term your involvement may have helped the family to continue with their day-to-day life without too much distress. However, you may have noticed that the relief only lasts a short while, until the OCD strikes again. You may also have noticed that OCD becomes more demanding the more you give in to it.

Use the space below to list the activities that OCD has drawn you into.

In addition to assisting with compulsions, OCD may have affected your life in other ways. You may have avoided leaving your child at a friend's, or you may have changed your own plans due to worries about the effects of OCD. Use the space below to detail the other ways in which OCD has affected your family. You may need to remind your child that it is OCD that causes these disruptions within the family, not the child.

Part B

HOW TO RECOVER FROM YOUR OCD

In this part of the book we are going to help you learn techniques to recover from your OCD. All of the strategies used in this section are based on cognitive behaviour therapy (CBT). You have already been introduced to this type of talking treatment in Chapter 4, so you know that it is the effective treatment used by professionals who treat OCD.

Chapter 7 helps you understand your anxious feelings, as understanding anxiety is an important first step in recovering from your OCD. Chapter 8 then helps you understand your difficulties with OCD in more detail. To do this you will learn how to keep an *OCD diary* and how to make an *OCD ladder*. You can then use these 'tools' to start to tackle your OCD problems by learning a technique called *exposure and response prevention*, or E/RP for short. This is the main technique that you will master to help you overcome your OCD.

Occasionally, you may come up against some difficulties. There is a question-and-answer section, which will give you advice on how to overcome any problems that you may encounter when trying to make progress.

Sometimes OCD makes you really worried about upsetting thoughts, and you might find it difficult to make progress until you have worked on these worries. There is a chapter to help you understand how common these types of thoughts are when you have OCD, and advice on how best to challenge and test these thoughts. You will also learn how to test whether your OCD thoughts are going to come true through the use of a technique called *behavioural experiments*.

Finally, once you have started to recover from OCD, you can learn how to maintain the gains that you have made, and what to do if OCD tries to reappear in your life!

Chapter 6

How to Use this Book to Change Your OCD

In the previous section you have learned what OCD is, how it can keep you caught in its trap, and about the treatment called CBT. The most powerful technique we use in CBT is a special sort of task called *exposure and response prevention* (E/RP). This is a psychological strategy that has been proven to work with OCD. Each E/RP task will help you understand and confront your OCD worries. Like all new skills it will involve practice and you will have to repeat tasks until you learn more about your OCD and your worries lessen. You may need to practise your E/RP exercises several times a day in order to make progress.

Obsessive compulsive disorder will make you feel frightened and want to avoid making any changes. It is therefore important to set time aside *each week* to fight your OCD. It may be helpful to use a timetable to schedule when you are going to practise your OCD tasks. You'll find a timetable in Chapter 11, 'Overcoming Difficulties'. It is recommended that the exercises in this workbook are completed in order, but you can repeat or return to sections if you want. After each chapter there is a chance to review what worked or did not work, and you can either continue working on that OCD task or set your next challenge.

Your OCD is very good at making you afraid to change anything! Because of this it is important to involve an adult helper to encourage you to fight your OCD symptoms. The 'Advice for parents or carers' sections in each chapter will assist your adult helper. The helper doesn't have to be a parent. They might be a guardian, carer or counsellor, or another

CHLOE

Chloe was very worried about germs, and wanted to wash all of her cutlery and plates before she used them. She was worried that if she didn't do this she would get very ill. She found it very difficult to start the first task, aimed at helping her on the road to recovery. She avoided doing the tasks by telling herself that 'it wouldn't work anyway', 'it was too risky to attempt', and that 'it was OK to continue doing her OCD rituals'. She always planned to start the tasks tomorrow, but tomorrow never came. Chloe discussed this avoidance with her mum and they decided to use the timetable to schedule in tasks to complete throughout the week. After each task they also scheduled a time to sit down and review the tasks, and a time to schedule in something that Chloe could look forward to doing to encourage her to want to continue facing her worries. This helped Chloe start to make changes.

important adult who knows you well and can support you in making changes even when you feel unsure or frightened. Remember that you *can* read those sections too. It may help to talk this section through with the person helping you so that you can plan each task until you become more confident in your ability to tackle your OCD successfully on your own. There are worksheets throughout the book to help you with your OCD challenges. These can all be photocopied.

MEASURING YOUR OCD

One thing that you may find helpful and interesting to do before you start to fight back against OCD is to complete a brief questionnaire (see the Appendix section). This questionnaire will provide you with a rough idea of how much the obsessions and compulsions are interfering in your life. It is helpful to complete this questionnaire once now (before you start to overcome OCD) and again when you finish working through all of the chapters in Part B of this book. This will allow you to compare the scores that you obtain, and to see whether your OCD symptoms have changed as a result of the work that you have done.

You need to score the questionnaire. You will be able to get a separate score for how much the compulsions and the obsessions are interfering in your life.

To score the compulsions part of the questionnaire, you will find six questions that ask:

- how much time you spend doing compulsions

- how much the compulsions get in the way of you doing things

- how upset you would feel if you were prevented from doing the compulsions

- how much you try to fight the compulsions

- how strong the feeling is that you have to carry out the compulsions, and

- how much you have been avoiding things, places or people because of the compulsions.

To get a score that will indicate how much the compulsions are interfering in your life, simply add up the numbers that you have circled for each of these questions. Put your score in the space provided below.

To score the obsession part of the questionnaire, you will find six questions that ask:

- how much time you spend thinking about the obsessions

- how much the thoughts get in the way of you doing things

- how much the thoughts bother you or upset you

- how hard you try to stop the thoughts or ignore them

- how much control you have over the thoughts, and

- how much you have been avoiding things, places or people because of the thoughts.

To get a score that will indicate how much the obsessions are interfering in your life, simply add up the numbers that you have circled for each of these questions. Put your score in the space provided below.

Compulsions interference score: _____

Obsessions interference score: _____

TOTAL interference score: _____

If your total score is 12 or more, it may be helpful for you to speak to your doctor about OCD. Take a copy of this questionnaire if you think that you have OCD but you are not sure. He or she may suggest that you see a clinical psychologist or a psychiatrist who may be able to help you further.

SUMMARY

- Each exercise is based on 'exposure and response prevention' (E/RP).

- Practise and the task will get easier for you.

- Use a timetable to help you organize when to do your OCD work.

- Review your progress frequently.

- Involve an adult helper.

- Use the questionnaire to measure how much your OCD is getting in the way of your life.

Now turn to the next chapter on page 69

ADVICE FOR PARENTS OR CARERS

Congratulations, you have been picked by your child to help use this workbook to fight OCD. This is a very important and significant task as OCD is very difficult to fight alone. One reason for this is that OCD encourages avoidance, and the more your child avoids confronting their fears, the more likely it is that he or she will continue having OCD symptoms. They have picked you to help them understand and fight their OCD using this workbook. Each chapter will include tasks for the child to complete, an opportunity to reflect and review what has been learned and to plan their next strategy. There are additional sections for you to read to give you ideas on how to support and encourage positive change.

If you are living with the child with OCD, then you have most likely experienced first-hand how frustrating and confusing OCD can be. For example, if your child has contamination fears then they may avoid touching door handles without washing their hands, but are carefree when it comes to the dog licking their face. OCD may make no sense to you, but to your child there is often a good rationale for why and how they engage in their rituals. However, they may not wish to share their reasoning with you as they may feel embarrassed, confused or frightened that their fears will then come true.

Do not blame yourself for the OCD either, it has not occurred because of anything you have or have not done. Try instead to practise seeing the OCD as something separate from your child, not something that they are doing to be deliberately difficult. Remember that it is the OCD that makes everyone upset.

HOW TO HELP

When using the book with your child it is important to have a collaborative approach. In short, you both need to decide and agree how much or little support is needed to complete the workbook exercises. It is important to strike a balance between helping your child take the lead if desired, or taking the lead yourself if your child agrees that this would be most helpful in getting them started.

Being supportive is essential. OCD is powerful in raising everyone's emotions, especially feelings of fear and anger. It is important to keep a non-blaming, non-judgemental attitude when supporting and encouraging your child. Do not criticize, become discouraged or negative. A positive approach is only going to encourage your child to be brave enough to make the changes they need to enable recovery. Use verbal praise frequently to reward progress, however small.

OCD recovery is rarely a continuous process, so expect there to be frequent relapses and times when your child wants to give up on attempts to fight their OCD. This is when praise and encouragement are essential.

When using this workbook, you may have to juggle several different roles. Look through the rest of this section with the child and discuss how you could be helpful.

Clarifier

Sometimes your child may need help in understanding how to complete the tasks. Sometimes their OCD fears and thoughts may interfere with their ability to make sense of the instructions or rationale for the tasks. Your role is to explain the importance and relevance of the task, and how to complete it.

Problem-solver

Sometimes the problems that your child's OCD cause may need creative solutions that require adapting the principal ideas of the task, and they may need your help in deciding how best to manage. Your child may need help learning how to manage and solve problems that arise.

Monitor

You may have a role in helping monitor your child's progress. This could include helping them with ratings for the tasks.

Reviewer

After each task has been completed, it is important that your child understands what they have learned from the task, and how to use this information to help challenge and change their OCD. Like a scientist, it is your job to help them make sense of the information they have generated and to use this to help them change their OCD thinking and behaviour, and to repeat or plan their next task. Together you may decide that it is time to move on to the next exercise, or to repeat the current exercise for longer.

Motivator

This role involves encouraging your child to tackle the tasks, and not to avoid confronting their fears. Avoidance can take many forms, and people with OCD are exceptionally good at avoiding changing their OCD behaviour due to their fear about what will happen if they do so. As a motivator you will need to think of individual ways that encourage your child to complete tasks. These may include using a timetable to schedule OCD practice time, arranging pleasurable activities after completing the OCD tasks, agreeing longer-term rewards which could be used to motivate your child to work hard on their OCD for a week, such as a trip out or treat. At times people with OCD may be quite perfectionist in their thinking and may need help completing tasks to a 'good enough' level, rather than giving up.

Advocate

At times your child will need help negotiating life's other challenges and how OCD impacts on their life outside of the home, such as with friends and at school. The final chapters of the book outline OCD and the bigger picture. This may be helpful in increasing your understanding of OCD in order to act as an advocate for your child. You may also need to represent your child if they need further help from professionals working in health and/or education.

SUMMARY

- Develop a collaborative and supportive relationship with your child to beat their OCD together.

- Decide together what roles you will take to be helpful, and remember that these might change over time.

- Reward progress, however small, especially with praise and encouragement.

- Set time aside to discuss progress and plan tasks.

- Remember, you are cross with the OCD, not with the affected child.

Chapter 7

Understanding the Role of Anxiety

This chapter will help you develop a good understanding of anxiety, how it can be measured, and its involvement in OCD. Understanding about anxiety is important, because it is one of the main feelings that helps to keep OCD going. You will learn what anxiety is, why we all experience it, and when it can be helpful and unhelpful. You will learn how to measure and record your own anxiety with an 'anxiety thermometer' as this will become an important tool in overcoming your OCD. This information will be valuable to you as we move into the next stage of fighting your OCD.

WHAT IS ANXIETY?

Anxiety is an uncomfortable feeling that includes worry, fear and apprehension. It is accompanied by a variety of thoughts and physical sensations. Anxiety occurs when we sense danger and it can help to protect us from physical harm by preparing the body to escape or avoid danger, or to defend itself. These reactions are sometimes referred to as the 'fight or flight' response.

This special anxiety response has always been useful for humans, even cavemen! For example, if a tiger was about to attack, anxiety would prepare a human to run away (take flight) or to find a way to kill the tiger (fight). However, the world today is less dangerous, and the threats that we face – such as handing in work on time or doing an exam – do not really need such a physical response.

THE PHYSICAL EFFECTS OF ANXIETY

The physical effects of anxiety include a rapid heart beat, quick breathing, tense muscles, shaking, upset stomach, sweating and headaches. When you sense danger your body's fight or flight mechanism will fire into action. Your senses will be sharpened to allow you to pay more attention to the threat that you could be facing. You breathe faster to provide extra oxygen to your muscles, and your heart works harder to pump this oxygenated blood to your muscles and away from other areas such as your stomach. This can cause you to feel as if you have 'butterflies' in your stomach or make you feel like you need to use the toilet. You may also notice your muscles becoming tense as they prepare themselves to act. These reactions can cause your body to heat up and you will sweat to prevent overheating.

Some people experience all of the above symptoms while others do not. Use Worksheet 7.1 on the next page to describe and understand your own experience of anxiety.

Worksheet 7.1

How anxiety affects me

Use the diagram below to show how anxiety affects you. Here are some suggestions to help get you started:

- Heart racing
- Tense muscles
- Sweating

- Dry mouth
- Shaking
- …

WHEN IS ANXIETY HELPFUL?

Anxiety is helpful when it acts to protect us from harm. For this to happen it must occur when there is a *real* danger. For example, if you were crossing a road and sensed a car speeding towards you, your anxiety would help you to move more quickly to avoid being run over.

Can you think of a time that anxiety has been helpful for you? Write it down in the space provided below.

WHEN IS ANXIETY UNHELPFUL?

Anxiety is unhelpful when there is no real danger. Unhelpful anxiety is like an alarm bell being triggered at the wrong time. This can happen if you think a situation is threatening when it is not. OCD tricks us by triggering anxiety when it is not needed. It encourages us to *overestimate* the likelihood and extent of danger, and to *underestimate* our ability to cope. There may be no real danger, or the danger may be so small that the anxiety response is not justified.

CAN ANXIETY HARM ME?

Despite the intense physical symptoms and worry that occurs with anxiety, feeling anxious has never hurt anyone. Even though your symptoms feel awful and frightening, they are simply extreme reactions of normal bodily sensations. At the moment it may feel as if your anxiety will go on forever unless you react with a compulsion. However, anxiety *does* pass on its own and usually lasts no longer than an hour. Although you may not believe this right now, you will have the chance to experience your own anxiety decreasing, without doing compulsions, as you progress through this book.

HABITUATION, OR 'GETTING USED TO' ANXIETY

Habituation is a word used to describe what happens when your body 'gets used to' an experience. It can happen in all sorts of situations. You may have noticed your body getting used to the temperature of water when you have been in a cold swimming pool. When you first get in you might feel so cold that you want to get back out, but if you stay in the pool for long enough your body becomes used to the temperature and no longer feels so cold. It has 'habituated' to the cool temperature.

It is also possible to habituate to anxiety. We know, from having helped other children and young people overcome their OCD, that everyone can habituate to their anxiety by practising to face their fear. This means that over time their anxiety does not feel so strong.

To habituate to anxiety caused by OCD, you practise experiencing anxiety without doing a compulsion. The more that you practise facing your anxiety, the less anxious you will feel and the quicker your anxiety will disappear.

We know that facing anxiety is tough, and because of this it can be helpful to learn how to face your anxiety in bite-size stages – a bit like easing yourself into a cold pool gradually. If you want to begin by just dipping your little toe into the pool of anxiety then that is okay.

Regardless of where you start you will get used to the different temperatures of your anxiety and learn that resisting compulsions is not as scary as you first thought. Before you start to do this, however, you will need to have a way to measure and record your own anxiety.

AN 'ANXIETY THERMOMETER'

The anxiety thermometer can be used to measure your feelings of anxiety. At the moment it may be hard to describe quite how difficult or anxiety-provoking a situation can be as you will be limited to words such as 'anxious', 'not anxious' or 'really anxious'. By using this scale you can be more sensitive to the different levels of anxiety. This will help you to rate how you feel with precision, and will also help you to monitor your anxiety over time and notice changes.

USING AN 'ANXIETY THERMOMETER' TO RATE HOW YOU FEEL ABOUT DOING A TASK

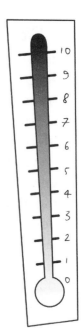

The anxiety thermometer is a 0–10 point scale, with 10 being the most anxious you have ever felt and 0 being the least anxious that you have ever felt. As an example, a 10 might be the equivalent of doing a parachute jump for someone who is afraid of heights, and a 0 might be lying on your bed and listening to relaxing music. The anxiety thermometer can be used to rate how hard it would be to stop or to change your compulsions. Take a look at the example below to see how this can work.

LYLA

Lyla had worrying obsessions about failing at school but felt that if she got ready for school in a certain order and time she could prevent this from happening. She had rituals around the way in which she washed and changed, and rules about starting again if the pattern was broken. When Lyla learned about her OCD and how to begin fighting it, she realized that some of her compulsions felt more frightening than others to change. She noticed that changing the order in which she dressed felt really scary – her heart raced even at the thought and she was certain that if she were to do this she would most definitely do badly at school. Lyla rated this as a 9 on her anxiety thermometer. However, the idea of changing one thing about the order in which she washed, for example washing her feet first instead of her face, felt less frightening. The thought worried her, but she felt that she would be able to just about manage it. Lyla rated that changing this compulsion would be a 4 on her anxiety thermometer.

USING AN 'ANXIETY THERMOMETER' TO RATE HOW YOU FEEL OVER TIME

The anxiety thermometer can also be used to measure your anxiety over time. For example, during her recovery Lyla bravely decided that she would decrease the time that she allowed herself to get ready for school by five minutes. Lyla rated this as a 5 out of 10 in terms of how anxious she felt about the task. When she completed the task she rated her anxiety as a 5, and felt very nervous. However, after 10 minutes it had come down to a 3 out of 10 and she felt more able to relax, and 5 minutes later it was back to a 0.

ANXIETY GRAPHS

With your new measure of anxiety it will be possible for you to plot your own graph and see how your anxiety changes over time.

Figure 6 shows what happens to your anxiety when you are caught in the OCD trap. When you experience an obsession your anxiety will rise and when you engage in a compulsion it will decrease, but each time you experience the worry your anxiety returns.

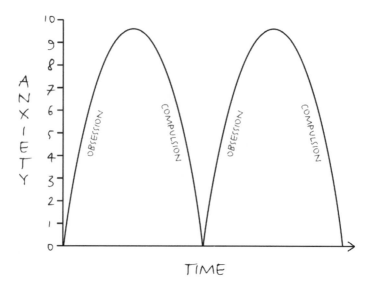

Figure 6 Caught in the OCD trap: anxiety remains

Figure 7 shows what happens to anxiety when you resist a ritual and habituate to your anxiety. When you resist a ritual, the anxiety lasts longer than it would if you had completed the ritual. However, it does not last forever and it does reduce. As the task is practised, the anxiety experienced lessens, until eventually you no longer feel the need to do a compulsion.

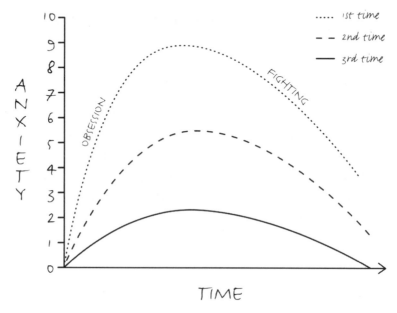

Figure 7 Fighting OCD: anxiety reduces with practice at resisting compulsions

When Lyla plotted what happened to her anxiety each time she practised the task of allowing an extra five minutes to get ready, the graph looked a lot like the example here. As you can see, the more she practised the task the easier it became and the less anxious she felt. *She habituated to her anxiety.*

In Chapter 8 of this book, 'What does My OCD Look Like?', you will get a chance to use the anxiety thermometer and anxiety graphs to help you fight your own OCD symptoms.

SUMMARY

- Anxiety is an uncomfortable feeling that includes worry, fear and distress.

- Anxiety cannot hurt you, and it does not last forever.

- Everyone can habituate or 'get used to anxiety' so that it passes.

- It involves physical changes that prepare your body for 'fight or flight'.

- Anxiety can be measured using an anxiety thermometer.

- OCD uses anxiety to keep you in the OCD trap.

Now turn to the next chapter on page 80

ADVICE FOR PARENTS AND CARERS

As you will have seen in earlier chapters, anxiety plays an important role in maintaining the OCD trap. Anxiety is a normal feeling, and is crucial in the face of real danger. For example, if you were crossing a road and noticed a car speeding towards you, you would experience the sensations of anxiety. Your heart would beat faster, your senses would be heightened and your muscles would be tense and ready for action. These sensations are vital to our survival as they prepare us to act. Often this will be by escaping the situation or by defending ourselves, responses known as 'fight or flight'.

Anxiety is probably present as part of the stress response, as it prepares the body for physical threat. However, the threats that we face in today's society do not always require the fight or flight response – for example relationship problems and difficulties at work – yet we can still experience the same anxiety response. When anxiety is experienced in situations that are not physically threatening, or is experienced in a way that is out of proportion to the actual threat, then it can be unhelpful. For example, anxiety may cause a person to escape a meeting at work if they are worried about making a mistake, even though that person might have prepared. Unhelpful anxiety is a component of OCD.

In the main section of this chapter your child can learn about anxiety and its importance in the OCD trap. He or she will be introduced to the 'anxiety thermometer', a 0–10 scale for helping them to measure and keep track of their own anxiety. At the top of this scale, a 10 would refer to the most anxiety that they have ever felt. A situation that made them frightened for their life might be a 10. At the bottom of the scale, a 0 would refer to the least anxious they have ever felt. They might feel a 0 when sitting listening to their favourite song.

You might find it useful to think about your own anxiety thermometer. What would be a 10 for you? Perhaps it is completing a parachute jump or having to defend yourself from an intruder? Maybe a 5 out of 10 would be giving a presentation at work and a 3 out of 10 speaking to someone you don't know very well. Each person's anxiety ratings will be different. Thinking about your own anxiety will also help you to think about how scary some of your child's OCD thoughts and behaviours feel to them. For them, not checking the light switch ten times may feel as threatening as seeing their parent held at knife-point.

It can feel difficult or strange to rate anxiety. Sometimes it is confusing to think about what rating to give your anxiety. Your child is likely to find this easier the more they practise. However, if they have difficulty – for example, if they rate everything as a 10 out of 10 – you can help them to search for anxiety cues. A 10 out of 10 anxiety rating is likely to be accompanied by signs that you can observe, such as their worried face and tense body. They may feel sweaty and distracted, or notice their heart racing and their stomach churning. As their anxiety reduces in intensity you may observe their body relax and their expression soften. In the main section of this book your child will have had the opportunity to think about the anxious sensations that most apply to them. Reviewing this information may help them to measure their anxiety. Measuring anxiety is difficult and not an exact science, so don't worry too much about being precise.

Having a way to measure anxiety also provides you and your child with a means to monitor their anxious feelings over time. This is important, as it will give your child the evidence they need to see that their anxiety *will* reduce over time without doing a compulsion. It will also allow them to see their levels of anxiety reducing as they progress through the tasks in this workbook.

Chapter 8

What does My OCD Look Like?

WHAT ARE MY OCD PROBLEMS?

The aim of this chapter is to begin to understand your OCD problems in more detail. In this chapter you will learn how to make a diary of your OCD compulsions and rate how much worry they cause you. Once you really understand your OCD worries, you will then be ready to progress on to the next chapters to start treatment.

Starting to think about all the behaviours that OCD makes you do could leave you feeling a little overwhelmed. It may seem like a huge task to record all of your rituals, especially if it feels as if you are doing something related to your OCD all day long. Don't worry, feeling that your OCD is out of your control is normal at this stage. Things will get better. This chapter helps you break your difficulties down into manageable chunks, so that you can start to be in control of making some small changes. One of the best ways of initially understanding your OCD problems is to keep a diary.

KEEPING AN OCD DIARY

Obsessive compulsive disorder is really good at keeping you busy making you do exactly what it wants you to do! It also tricks you into thinking that your problems are so big that you will never be able to record all of them. OCD is wrong.

You can use Worksheet 8.1 to start to record your OCD compulsions. You may need to photocopy the worksheet to record more of your OCD difficulties.

Sometimes you may find that you do many of your compulsions almost like a habit, but you need to record these too. You could get your helper to assist you in recording your habits, and to help you decide whether some of your habits are actually OCD. It may be worth recording your OCD for a few days, or up to a week. The important thing is for you to build up a picture of what your OCD looks like. Below is a case example that will help you understand how to complete worksheet 8.1.

My OCD diary

Over a week, use this table to make a record of what OCD makes you do, and how many times each day it makes you do it.

When was it?	What did OCD make you do?	For how long?

SAM

Sam, aged 16 years, was very worried that something bad would happen to him and his family. He spent a long time checking that the electrical appliances had been switched off correctly, and that doors and windows had been firmly locked. He was frightened that if something bad did happen, he would feel responsible if he had not carried out his checking rituals correctly. He also believed that even numbers were 'good' numbers, and that odd numbers were 'unlucky'. This belief made him want to check only an even number of times. He spent much of the day checking things in his home an even number of times, or until it 'felt right', often repeating the checking if he still felt uncomfortable.

Figure 8 shows an example from Sam's worksheet, 'My OCD diary'. When you are ready, use Worksheet 8.1 to make a record of what OCD makes you do, and how many times each day you have to do your rituals. You could spend about a week doing this.

When was it?	What did OCD make you do?	For how long?
Tuesday night 9.15	Touch the toaster, kettle, oven and light switch in order before going up the stairs to bed. Continue until each item has been touched twice or feels right.	4 minutes
9.19	Touch the hall light switch at the bottom and top of the stairs. Carry on until switches have been touched 4 times or until it feels right.	2 minutes
9.21	Touch switches on stereo, TV, clock in bedroom. Stop when the switches have been touched 6 times or until it feels right.	4 minutes

Figure 8 Sam's OCD diary

MAKING AN OCD LADDER

Once you have used Worksheet 8.1 to really understand what your OCD makes you do, it is time to make your own *OCD ladder*. This is just a list of your OCD compulsions, put in an order to show how frightened or upset you think they will make you feel when you even think about changing them. (You will need this for your E/RP exercises in the next chapter.)

You learned to rate your anxiety using an 'anxiety thermometer' in Chapter 7. You will now need to use that thermometer to rate your OCD symptoms.

From your diary you will have a list of OCD behaviours. Some are probably very upsetting and difficult to stop, and others are probably a bit easier. You may have lots and lots of OCD behaviours, and wonder how you have time to do anything else. The aim of this task is to pick between eight and ten OCD behaviours that you would really like to change. They need to include the compulsion you think will be easiest to change and the one you think will be the most difficult to change.

If you find it difficult to rate your anxiety using the anxiety thermometer don't worry about it – make a best guess, or start by giving your rituals a general rating of 'low', 'medium' or 'high'. Working with your helper might make it a bit easier than doing it on your own.

If you have given two tasks the same rating, try to decide which would be more difficult to change, and give that a higher rating. The highest item on your ladder should be the situation that triggers your highest levels of anxiety and fear.

Don't worry if you have more OCD behaviours off the list than on the list. Once you have learned how to manage your OCD with the behaviours on the list, you can use these skills to make further OCD ladders and tackle other OCD problems if necessary. Once you start your E/RP exercises some symptoms may just get better on their own, and other new rituals may need to be added to your ladder if they become very bothersome.

You will therefore need to keep your OCD ladder up to date, so that old symptoms can be re-scored, and new symptoms added as needed. Worksheet 8.2 has an OCD ladder for you to complete.

Making my OCD ladder

Choose up to ten compulsions from your diary to work on. Write them down in the column under OCD difficulties. Rate each OCD difficultly on the scale 0–10, by thinking how anxious or worried you would be if you could not do the compulsion. How hard would it be to stop?

	OCD DIFFICULTIES	ANXIETY RATING 0–10
1		
2		
3		
4		
5		
6		
7		
8		
9		
10		

OLIVER

Oliver, age 11 years, was bullied at school, and worries about bullies got linked into OCD rituals. He started to have thoughts that the bullies were magically taking over his mind and his home. In order to stop this happening, he avoided any object that could have, either directly or indirectly, been in contact with the bullies. At first he avoided taking anything home from school that he thought the bullies had touched. This included his books, school bag and glasses. He disliked contact with his mother's handbag, as she often carried it when she met him from school, or went on parent evenings. Oliver then started worrying about places that he had sat at home. He thought that these places could be contaminated as he or his friends had sat there after contact with the bullies. The computer table was particularly difficult, as he had opened nasty e-mails from the bullies, and often put his school books and bag on the table. Things had become so difficult that he found it hard to wear his school uniform, and was constantly making excuses to avoid attending school. Whenever he heard the bullies' names, he had to repeat 'I'm safe' to himself up to ten times, or until it felt just right. The most upsetting part for Oliver was that he was now unable to touch his favourite comfort toy that he had had since childhood, which made him feel very sad. Take a look at Figure 9 to see his OCD ladder.

OCD DIFFICULTIES		ANXIETY RATING 0-10
1	Repeating 'I'm safe' (10 times) whenever I hear the name Charlie	9
2	Not wearing school uniform	9
3	Avoiding home computer chair	8
4	Avoiding sitting on lounge chairs	8
5	Not able to touch school books	7
6	Not able to touch school bag	6
7	Not able to touch glasses	5
8	Avoiding touching favourite cuddly toy	4
9	Avoiding wearing school trainers	3
10	Avoiding touching mum's handbag	2

Figure 9 Oliver's OCD ladder

DECIDING WHERE TO START

Now that you have your completed OCD ladder, you need to decide which OCD difficulty you would like to work on in your first E/RP exercise. There are several things that you and your parent or carer may like to consider.

It is often wise to pick the OCD difficulty that is at the *bottom* of your ladder and has the lowest anxiety rating. This should make it a bit easier to confront your anxiety (because it is not as high as some others) and therefore makes it more likely that your first experiment will be successful. You will also learn how to conduct E/RP exercises, and can use these skills for the more difficult behaviours in your ladder later on.

Sometimes there may be behaviours on your ladder that you really would like to change, maybe because it takes up a lot of your time, or it gets in the way of you doing your favourite activity. It is OK to start with this OCD difficulty, as long as it has a low level of anxiety, a rating of no more than say 4 or 5.

In the case described below, Oliver decided that his first experiment would be touching his favourite comfort toy (rating of 4). He picked this as he missed having it on his bed at night. He felt sad and angry that the OCD had made him feel that the bullies had contaminated his toy, and that it was too risky to touch. This really motivated him to confront his fears.

WHAT SHOULD I DO NEXT?

Once you have completed the exercises in this chapter, it is important to think about what you have learned about your OCD difficulties, and to have a plan of action to help you progress with the later experiments. Worksheet 8.3 will help you assess what you have learned and plan your next move against OCD. Once you have completed this, it may be helpful to talk it through with your parent or carer.

Making an action plan

What are the most important things that you have learned about your OCD difficulties from doing the exercises in Chapter 8?

From your OCD ladder, which OCD compulsion have you chosen to work on first?

Why have you chosen this compulsion?

How will your life be better if you do not have to do this compulsion?

What difficulties might come up when you work on your chosen OCD compulsion?

How could you overcome these?

SUMMARY

- Keep a diary of your OCD rituals.

- Chose up to ten compulsions from your diary to work on.

- Make an OCD ladder by rating your compulsions on a 0–10 scale.

- The rating is how anxious it would make you feel if you did *not* do your compusion.

- Choose one compulsion to start your E/RP exercises.

- Review what you have learned and develop your action plan.

- Involve your mum or dad (or other helper) if you get stuck.

Now turn to the next chapter on page 94

ADVICE FOR PARENTS OR CARERS

The aim of this chapter is to help your child understand his or her OCD difficulties, and to build an OCD treatment ladder to use throughout the following chapters. Making a list of compulsions can be quite difficult for someone with OCD as they often feel that they have too many difficulties to capture on paper, or that their OCD worries get in the way of writing down their problems. If they do find it difficult to make a list, help them break their problems down into manageable chunks. For example, spend one day just recording bedtime rituals, then the next day recording rituals that happen around breakfast. Encourage your child to continue doing this until they feel that their diary really captures their difficulties.

Next they are asked to pick up to ten compulsions for their ladder. It is important that these capture the range of their difficulties, not just the ones that are most easy or difficult to change. Try to support and encourage them, and remember that what you think is the most irritating or upsetting OCD behaviour may not correspond with your child's view. If you do not agree about this, it is the child's view that is most relevant for treatment.

It can be difficult to use the anxiety thermometer to rate OCD difficulties. Some young people are able to rate the most difficult and most easy OCD compulsion to change, but find that many of the rest fall somewhere in the middle. Help them order their compulsions by asking them something like 'Out of compulsion A or B, which one would make you the most upset or worried if you had to stop doing it?' If a child finds this exercise difficult, you could encourage them to write each compulsion onto a separate piece of paper, and move them around the table to get them into the correct order. You could then rate each task, and transfer the information to Worksheet 8.2.

The final task of the chapter is for your child to pick a target compulsion for his or her first E/RP experiment, outlined in the next chapter. Read 'Deciding where to start' to help you guide your child if they cannot decide. Remember that the first experiment needs to be *achievable*, in order for the child to build up confidence, motivation and skills in fighting their OCD.

SUMMARY

- Problem solve any difficulties your child has when completing the OCD diary.

- If needed, help your child with ratings to construct an OCD ladder.

- Discuss with your child which OCD compulsion to initially work on.

- Review your child's action plan.

Chapter 9 **Designing Exposure and Response Prevention Exercises**

WHAT IS EXPOSURE AND RESPONSE PREVENTION (E/RP)?

The main CBT tool that you will need to learn to fight your OCD is called 'exposure and response prevention', or E/RP for short. We know that E/RP is one of the most effective tools for fighting OCD.

- *Exposure* means facing your OCD fears until your anxiety naturally goes down. You will need to expose yourself to your feared object, action or thought. For example, Ashley (who we'll meet later) has a fear about touching his front door handle without tissue paper. Doing an exposure task would require him to touch the 'contaminated' door handle until his anxiety decreases. Exposure is best done in a gradual manner, which is why we have encouraged you to rate the level of difficulty for doing the tasks on your OCD ladder.

- *Response prevention* means not engaging in any compulsions or avoidance behaviours when facing your OCD worries. For example, Ashley would be required not to use tissue paper to touch the door and not to wash his hands after touching the front door handle.

In order to get better you will need to regularly and repeatedly face your OCD fears and not respond to them or avoid them. You will then become used to them, and your anxiety will lessen. This is called 'habituation', which you read about in Chapter 7. To remind you of what this means, we have included the following bungee jump example. If you did a bungee jump, the first time you jumped your anxiety level might be really high (say 9 out of 10). If you repeated the jump say 15 times, it would get easier and easier each go until your anxiety was only 0 or 1 on the rating scale. In short, practice and confronting your fear many times leads to a reduction in your fear level.

You can use your OCD ladder to help you pick tasks for your E/RP exercises. When carrying out E/RP exercises, your aim is to tolerate your feelings of anxiety, and to stay with the experience until your anxiety level significantly goes down.

DESIGNING YOUR FIRST E/RP EXERCISE

You are now ready to plan your first E/RP exercise. You have already picked the OCD difficulty that you would like to change. Now you need to have an E/RP action plan to help you change it. Having a good imagination can really help with this!

Try to think of any way that you can do the *opposite* of what OCD would normally have you do. Some tasks will be easier than others. Your parent (or other helper) may need to be involved at this point, if you are finding it too difficult to think of ways to change your behaviour.

The best way of doing your E/RP work is to stop doing the compulsion completely. In the case of Ashley, this would simply mean touching the doorhandle (exposing himself to his fears of contamination), and not doing any compulsions (washing his hands, or using tissue). Complete Worksheet 9.1 by taking a look at your OCD ladder, and deciding what you would need to do to break your OCD rules.

How to break my OCD rules

Write the steps of your OCD ladder in the left-hand column. In the right-hand column write out your OCD plan of action. Try to think of any way that you can do the *opposite* of what OCD would normally have you do.

Your OCD ladder	How I will break my OCD rules

LISA

Lisa, 15 years, is very worried about catching germs when she is eating her meals. She spends a long time washing and re-washing her plates and cutlery before she uses them, as she thinks that this will protect her from catching germs. She can wash each item 10 times, and this can sometimes take up to an hour of her time. She is starting to lose interest in eating, and consequently is losing weight, as she feels so distressed about her cleaning compulsions.

LEARNING TO BREAK OCD'S RULES

Sometimes it may seem far too difficult to just stop your compulsions, even in a gradual way. Although this is your aim, to start with you may need to learn a variety of strategies to weaken and break your OCD rules. Here are some ideas.

Delay the ritual

How long can you make OCD wait before you do the ritual? For example, if you feel that you need to check a switch right now, can you delay doing this for, say, two minutes? Once you can do this, gradually increase the time delay.

Shorten the ritual

Try to limit the amount of time it takes you to do your ritual. For example, if you need to wash your hands for five minutes, cut the time down by one minute on each E/RP exercise.

Do your ritual differently

If you have to do your ritual in a certain way, try doing it in a different way. For example, if you have to do your ritual a certain number of times, change the number a bit. If you have to do the ritual until 'it feels right', stop when it still feels a bit wrong. It can be fun to think of different ways to 'mess up' the rules!

Do your ritual in a different place

If you find it hard to stop your ritual at home, try stopping it in another place first – such as at school, around at grandparents, or at a friend's home.

If you are still finding it difficult, it may be worth breaking the task down into more manageable steps. Figure 10 shows an example of how to break a task into manageable steps from Lisa's workbook. Here the ultimate aim is for her to be able to take a fork from the drawer without washing it at all.

Item from your OCD ladder	Anxiety 1–10
Taking fork from drawer, and only washing it three times, and only taking a maximum of 5 minutes	
Taking fork from drawer and washing it twice	
Taking fork from drawer and washing it once	
Taking fork from drawer and using water, not washing-up liquid, to wash it	
Taking fork from drawer and wiping once with a damp cloth	
Taking fork from drawer and not washing it	

Figure 10 Lisa's small OCD exposure steps

> ### REMEMBER
> In order to get better you will still need to eventually stop your compulsion completely. If you can manage it, this is the best place to start.

DOING YOUR FIRST E/RP EXERCISE

By now you should have a really detailed plan to work with. You have picked an OCD difficulty from your ladder, and have designed what your first E/RP exercise will be. You are now ready to complete your first exercise! Remember that you will need to do this again and again, as the more times you repeat the task, the easier it will become and the quicker your anxiety will reduce.

Worksheet 9.2 is handy to use when conducting your E/RP exercises. You will need to photocopy more of this sheet, or use it as a template for making your own.

You can complete the tasks as many times as you want, the more often the better. In fact it may be helpful to keep practising the tasks even when they are no longer causing you any anxiety, to really keep your anxiety under control. Only when you feel that your anxiety has significantly reduced – and that you are able to resist the compulsion – should you move on to planning and exposing yourself to a new target from your OCD ladder.

A step-by-step guide to completing your first E/RP exercise

- Step 1. Use Worksheet 9.2 to write down your chosen difficulty from your OCD ladder, and your E/RP exercise designed to expose you to your fears.

- Step 2. Rate how anxious you feel about not doing what OCD wants you to do, using your 'anxiety thermometer'.

- Step 3. Decide what your parent or carer can do to help you.

- Step 4. Start your E/RP exercise.

- Step 5. Rate your feeling of anxiety with the 'anxiety thermometer' every few minutes. Your aim is to record it until it comes right down.

- Step 6. Keep repeating this task for as many trials as it takes to stop causing you anxiety.

- Step 7. Re-rate your anxiety level on your OCD ladder.

✓

My exposure and response prevention (E/RP) exercise

What is OCD telling you to do?						
What is your E/RP exercise going to be?						
Rate how you feel about not doing what OCD wants (0–10).						
What can your parent or carer do to help?						
Record below what happens to your feelings of anxiety						
Trial	Your exercise is?	1 min	5 mins	15 mins	30 mins	60 mins
Now rate again how you feel about not doing what OCD wants (0–10).						

LUCIA

Lucia's OCD started to interfere with her life when she was studying for exams. She started to worry that if she looked at certain letters while working, then she would fail her exams. She therefore avoided looking at any letters that she associated with failure, which included the letters D, E, F and U. She would spend hours covering up letters on items in her bedroom and in her textbooks, and repeating positive letters (A, B, C) every time she caught sight of her feared letters. Figure 11 shows an example from Lucia's workbook when she completed her first E/RP experiment.

What is OCD telling you to do?
To cover up letters D, E, F, U on my computer keyboard

What is your E/RP exercise going to be?
To look at the keyboard, and not to cover any letters or repeat the letter A, B, C

Rate how you feel about not doing what OCD wants (0–10).
7/10

What can your parent or carer do to help?
Prompt me to record my anxiety at the various time slots

Record below what happens to your feelings of anxiety

Trial	Your exercise is?	1 min	5 mins	15 mins	30 mins	60 mins
1	**To use the computer at home, and not to cover up the letters D, E, F, U when I am typing**	8	7	7	3	2
2		6	5	3	3	1
3		5	3	2	1	0

Now rate again how you feel about not doing what OCD wants (0–10)
1/10

Figure 11 Lucia's exposure and response prevention exercise

UPDATING YOUR OCD LADDER

Once you start to conduct your E/RP exercises you will find that your anxiety ratings on your ladder change. It is important to keep your ladder up to date, so that you can accurately plan further tasks. You will need to use the 'anxiety thermometer' to re-rate your anxiety after you have finished several trials of working on one difficulty. You can use the ladder on Worksheet 9.3.

Updating my OCD ladder

Copy down your OCD compulsions from your previous ladder (Worksheet 8.2) that are still worrying you, and any new compulsions that might have started to bother you. Write them down in the column under OCD compulsions. Again rate each OCD compulsion on the scale 0–10, by thinking how anxious or worried you would be if you could not do the compulsion. How hard would it be to stop?

	OCD DIFFICULTIES	ANXIETY RATING 0–10
1		
2		
3		
4		
5		
6		
7		
8		
9		
10		

WHAT SHOULD I DO NEXT?

Once you have completed your first E/RP experiment, think about what you have learned and what you need to do next in order to continue fighting your OCD. Answer the questions on Worksheet 9.4, and if useful, discuss these with your parent.

Worksheet 9.4

What progress have I made?

These questions can help you think about your progress. You may want to answer them after each E/RP task. Asking yourself these questions will help you to think about how far you have come. It will also help you to problem-solve difficulties, and recognize when tasks are too easy or too hard.

What was my E/RP exercise?

What went well?

Did my anxiety decrease over time?

Did I do anything to reduce my anxiety during the task (such as another ritual, avoiding something, distracting myself)

What did not go as well as I had hoped? How could I do things differently next time?

What did I learn about my OCD by doing the E/RP exercise?

Have I rewarded myself for my successes?

What do I need to do next to help me recover from my OCD?

SUMMARY

- Decide which OCD difficulty from your ladder you are going to tackle first.

- Design your first E/RP exercise.

- Conduct your first E/RP exercise, and record changes in your anxiety ratings.

- Repeat this exercise several times, until your anxiety rating is very low or 0. This may take a couple of days or it may take up to a week.

- Update your difficulties on your OCD ladder.

- Review what you have learned.

- Plan your next E/RP exercise.

Now turn to the next chapter on page 110

ADVICE FOR PARENTS OR CARERS

It is important to understand the rationale for E/RP exercises as this is the foundation of treatment. Read the section 'What is exposure and response prevention'. In short, each E/RP exercise deliberately produces anxiety that your child must tolerate without doing any compulsions. Your child will need to use their OCD ladder to design tasks that expose them to their OCD fears, and prevent them from engaging in their usual compulsions or avoidance. Your child may need help in designing these E/RP exercises.

When conducting E/RP tasks, it is essential that your child continue with each exercise until the anxiety comes down. This can initially take up to an hour, but will get quicker over several trials. You may have a role in helping them rate and record their anxiety using the 'anxiety thermometer'.

They will need lots of encouragement to resist engaging in their compulsions, as compulsions are so powerful due to the short-term relief they provide from anxious feelings. However, by completing a compulsion your child will not learn that anxious feelings subside naturally over time, and that there is nothing to fear when they do not engage in compulsions. This is a crucial lesson to learn: only when your child is able to tolerate the anxiety without their compulsions will true recovery start to occur.

It is also essential that your child does not introduce another ritual or avoidance behaviour to help manage the anxiety. For example, your child may engage in a mental ritual such as counting, which you would not be able to notice, but may serve the same function for them as a compulsion that you could see (e.g. washing). Alternatively, they may avoid situations during the E/RP task, which ultimately will maintain their OCD worries. Discuss these behaviours with your child when reviewing Worksheet 9.4, and problem-solve any difficulties together.

As E/RP exercises are difficult to complete, it is worth giving lots of encouragement and praise for attempts at these tasks to encourage motivation. Take a look at your child's re-ratings on their OCD ladder and praise any decrease in anxiety scores, however small. Remember that scores are unlikely to change unless your child has specifically focused on them with an E/RP task. It is also worth planning small treats that encourage your child to continue working to beat the OCD.

Furthermore, don't forget to spend time paying attention to other positive aspects of your child's life, not just their OCD.

SUMMARY

- Understand the rationale for E/RP exercises.

- If requested, help your child to design their E/RP tasks.

- If requested, help your child rate their anxiety every 2–3 minutes throughout their E/RP task.

- Set time aside to review progress.

- Tackle and problem-solve any difficulties.

- Reward any positive changes, however small.

- Remember to focus on other positive aspects of your child and his or her behaviour, not just their OCD.

Chapter 10

Making Progress with Exposure and Response Prevention Exercises

By now you will be familiar with the way to do E/RP exercises. If things have gone well, you can use this knowledge to tackle the rest of the difficulties on your OCD ladder, in much the same way. If problems have occurred, take a look at Chapter 11, 'Overcoming Difficulties'.

You will need to gradually tackle each difficulty on your ladder in the order you have rated them, starting with the easiest first (unless there is anything that you are particularly motivated to tackle). This will mean that the further you go up your ladder the harder the tasks will seem to become.

Remember that you must keep facing your fears, until your anxiety levels drop. You must not introduce any other rituals or avoidance behaviours, as this will just keep your problems going. The more that you practise, the easier the tasks will get. It is important to practise an E/RP exercise each day.

Do not move on to a new OCD compulsion until your worry associated with your current difficulty significantly lessens. We recommend that you get it down to at least 2 out of 10 before going on to the next one.

HOW TO DO MORE EXPOSURE AND RESPONSE PREVENTION (E/RP) EXERCISES

Just to remind you, here is a step-by-step guide for completing your E/RP exercises with the rest of the items on your ladder.

A step-by-step guide to progressing with E/RP

- Step 1. Choose an OCD difficulty with an anxiety rating slightly higher than your previous exercise.

- Step 2. Design your E/RP exercise.

- Step 3. Conduct your E/RP exercise, rating your anxiety using the 'anxiety thermometer'.

- Step 4. Do not introduce any new compulsions or ways of avoiding facing your anxiety.

- Step 5. Continue with the task until your anxiety levels drop to very low, at least 2 out of 10 but ideally 0.

- Step 6. Practise the same E/RP exercise several times each day if you can, until it gets easier.

- Step 7. Review your progress.

- Step 8. Re-rate your OCD difficulties on your ladder.

- Step 9. Make plans for further action.

MAKING SENSE OF YOUR FINDINGS

You should notice that your ratings of anxiety slowly decrease over time. This may take about an hour the first time that you do an E/RP exercise. However, as you practise over and over again, your anxiety levels will drop more quickly. This is why you will need to continue doing the same exercise over and over again.

To monitor these changes you may like to plot your own anxiety graphs. You read about these in Chapter 7 on page 75. You can use Worksheet 10.1 as a guide on how to plot your own anxiety graphs.

My anxiety graphs

- Choose an ER/P challenge that you are working on.
- Use the table below to record your anxiety over time.
- Use the graph below to plot these results. Use a different pen for each trial of your task so that you can easily see changes in your anxiety.

Trial number	Your experiment is?	1 min	5 mins	15 mins	30 mins	60 mins
1						
2						
3						

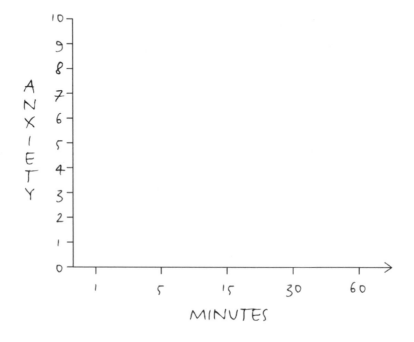

Before learning about OCD and how it works, you were using compulsions to try to make your anxiety feel more manageable. Can you now see that compulsions actually make the OCD and the anxiety stronger? We hope you find that your anxiety decreases naturally without you doing your compulsions. Therefore there is no need for your OCD! Keep practising, as each E/RP exercise will get easier over time, and each E/RP exercise will help you to get rid of OCD for good!

WHAT TO DO IF YOU GET STUCK

When you start tackling compulsions at the top of your ladder, you may feel like giving up, as they seem too difficult or distressing to tackle. If this happens, take a break from your E/RP exercises for a week, and plan lots of nice activities to celebrate how much progress you have made to date. Towards the end of the week start planning your most difficult E/RP task. Keep reminding yourself that you have beaten OCD before, and you can do it again. Plan something to do that you enjoy once you have completed the hardest E/RP exercises.

WHAT SHOULD I DO IF OTHERS ARE INVOLVED IN MY OCD?

It is common that others might get tangled up in your OCD, especially parents or brothers and sisters. You may be asking them frequently for reassurance about your OCD worries. Gaining reassurance often makes you feel better in the short term, as it gives you comfort that you haven't broken OCD's rules. However, this comfort rarely lasts for long.

Whenever the doubts reappear you will start to feel worried again and you will need further reassurance. Anyone who gives you reassurance has now become part of your OCD problem. Whenever worries arise you will constantly seek further reassurance in order to feel better. This is a vicious cycle that you and they will need to break.

Similarly, you may be asking family members to avoid touching objects or doing certain activities. They will need to gradually break OCD's rules, and stop doing what OCD wants them to do. When they do this, you will be able to see that the anxiety this causes will go away by itself. It's really important to make sure that your OCD ladder and E/RP exercises include other people changing *their* behaviours that maintain *your* OCD.

When family members start to challenge your OCD by not becoming involved in rituals, you may initially start to feel angry. Focus on directing your anger towards beating your OCD instead of on to members of your family.

WHAT SHOULD I DO NEXT?

It is important to take time to think about what you are learning. When you have conducted several trials of E/RP and completed Worksheet 9.2 on page 101, you can start to compare your scores over time. Also do not forget to re-rate items on your OCD ladder using Worksheet 9.3 on page 104. This will help you to monitor your progress and assess any obstacles that are getting in the way of change.

Check how much you are involving others in your compulsions, and ensure that you design your E/RP tasks to gradually cut back on their involvement. Spend time each week reviewing your progress and planning your next challenge against OCD.

SUMMARY

- Use your experience to pick your next E/RP exercise from your ladder.

- Watch your anxiety come down over time.

- Gradually work *up* your ladder.

- Problem-solve your difficulties with one of your parents or a helper if you get stuck.

- Repeatedly asking for reassurance will only *strengthen* your OCD.

- If others are involved in your OCD compulsions, ensure that your E/RP exercises take this into account.

Now turn to the next chapter on page 120

ADVICE FOR PARENTS OR CARERS

Your child's aim is to gradually work from the bottom to the top of their OCD ladder, targeting their OCD difficulties using E/RP exercises. For each exercise it is important that your child sticks with the task until their anxiety decreases to a rating of 2 or less for a couple of minutes. Telling your child to 'do it until it becomes boring' often works. If your child's symptoms are reducing, continue with this method. If problems arise, consult the following chapters for ideas on how to help resolve them.

Your child may need less input from you as their experience in conducting E/RP exercises grows. If this is the case, allow them to independently learn and practise the skills to manage their own symptoms. As they reach tasks towards the top of their ladder, they may find it more difficult to choose and complete their E/RP exercises. This is because these tasks cause the most anxiety, and hence avoidance. You will need to be more active in providing encouragement, praise and support at this point. Remember that any small changes are big steps towards overcoming OCD.

Once you start to see some improvement in your child's symptoms through them doing E/RP exercises, you may wish them to progress quickly by moving on to other items on their ladder. It is important to be patient and to continue the work at your child's own pace. Do not expect that they can manage to change behaviours before they have been targeted as specific E/RP exercises, even if they are particularly upsetting for you.

WHEN OCD INVOLVES YOU

It is common that people with OCD involve others in their compulsions or avoidance behaviours. This is called 'accommodating OCD'. You may have taken responsibility for doing some of the compulsions, you are probably going along with some of OCD's demands, or perhaps you are giving your child excessive amounts of reassurance. For example, your child may ask repeatedly for your reassurance as to whether they have touched something they perceive to be contaminated. You may have to repeat phrases in a certain way, or be banned from using items in the house, or parts of the home. Any or all of these ways of becoming involved in your child's OCD are really understandable. However, it is important to be able to learn how to remove yourself (and other family members) from being involved in the OCD.

LOUIE

Louie's fear of contamination lead him to become upset if family members used forks in the house (as the prongs were seen as excessively dirty). In order to accommodate his fears, all family members were involved in rituals to clean the forks, and place them prongs down in the drawer. Cleaning rituals were conducted if Louie thought that the fork had been in contact with anything. Certain areas of the kitchen were avoided. Family members were requested to wash their hands if they even looked at a fork. No one was allowed to use a fork to eat, and all meals were consumed using spoons only.

All of these difficulties were rated on Louie's OCD ladder, and E/RP tasks were designed that involved the gradual withdrawal of family members from Louie's compulsions. Initially Louie learned to tolerate his anxiety when family members placed forks prongs upwards in the drawer. The family's involvement in cleaning rituals was then gradually stopped. The final task on Louie's ladder was for the family to eat a meal using forks. At times Louie became distraught about any changes in his family's behaviour, which led to outbursts of foul language. He agreed with his family that they should remind him that they are all fighting his OCD together, and encourage him to go to his room for five minutes to calm down. Although it was a challenge, it was important that family members followed through with the E/RP exercises, and did not give in to OCD's demands.

HOW TO WITHDRAW FROM OCD'S DEMANDS

As you are probably aware, people with OCD can be very persuasive or demanding as they are so worried about the consequences of not doing their compulsions. It is therefore understandable that you have taken the option of 'accommodating OCD', since it reduces distress and prevents arguments in the short term. You will know that going along with OCD will stop any demands for a short period, and will relieve your child's anxiety for a short time. In the longer

term, however, it reinforces the idea that your child's anxiety can only be managed if you are involved in their compulsions. This creates a vicious circle with you central to maintaining your child's struggle with OCD.

The final goal is not to accommodate your child's compulsions and avoidance behaviours. However, you will have to make a decision as to how you gradually achieve this. Any change in your response to OCD's demands will cause distress to your child. Therefore you need to agree together how you can untangle yourself from accommodating OCD. It is worth using the child's ladder to help you plan a graded withdrawal from your child's OCD.

For example, if an item on the OCD ladder involves you giving reassurance, plan an E/RP exercise not to involve you. If you are caught up in not using items or rooms in the house, ensure that these are on your child's OCD ladder and targeted for E/RP. Remember to only expect changes on OCD compulsions that your child has worked on using E/RP.

You will need to have a plan for how to manage your child's distress. It is likely that if you do not accommodate OCD your child will feel very anxious. This feeling of being out of control could be displayed in a variety of ways, including verbal or physical aggression. Agree with your child how you intend to respond to their OCD demands, and stick to it. Use discipline consistently to ensure that your child knows that there are agreed consequences to their aggressive behaviour. Keep in mind that it is the OCD that you are angry with, and although it may be difficult, withdrawing gradually from its demands will only weaken its hold on you and your child.

WHAT TO DO ABOUT REASSURANCE SEEKING

Frequently young people with OCD involve others by asking for excessive reassurance. This may be about whether something is clean enough, whether they have touched a feared object, or whether something worrying is going to happen. It is likely that you will be repeating things over and over again using the same words. You will need to discuss this with your child and agree a plan of action.

Your child will need to resist their urge to ask for reassurance, in order to discover that their anxiety lessens over time. You will need to agree how to respond to excessive requests for reassurance. Initially it may help to devise a rule that you will respond once, and then ignore any further requests. Alternatively, it may be helpful to agree a phrase you can use that reminds the child that they are starting the pattern of reassurance seeking – something like 'What does OCD want now?' or 'I am not going to answer to OCD'.

SUMMARY

- Continue supporting, praising and motivating your child to attempt tasks, especially towards the top of their OCD ladder.

- Assess how much you, or other people, are involved in your child's OCD.

- Agree how to respond to excessive requests for reassurance that ultimately maintain OCD.

- Tackle any involvement you or other family members have in OCD through E/RP exercises.

- Remember to be patient, and expect only the OCD behaviours that have been worked on through E/RP exercises to change.

Chapter 11

Overcoming Difficulties

It is quite common to come up against problems when you are doing your E/RP exercises. This chapter uses a question-and-answer format to help you understand the most common difficulties that arise, and it gives you some ideas on how to overcome them.

QUESTIONS AND ANSWERS

I never get around to doing my E/RP exercises – what will help?

This is a common difficulty. OCD has made you afraid for a long time, and you may have got a little bit used to having OCD in your life. Maybe you have started to tell yourself that it's OK to keep doing your rituals, or that you don't really need to change things as OCD is keeping you safe.

Remind yourself that OCD is *not* your friend. Instead it makes you anxious, worried, and controls your life. It is helpful to challenge your thoughts about OCD by saying to yourself 'I am going to get OCD out of my life.'

Using a timetable to plan when you are going to conduct your E/RP exercises is also a helpful strategy. Worksheet 11.1 gives a template, but you may wish to use a home calendar, diary or mobile phone organizer instead. Once you have committed to doing an E/RP exercise, don't make excuses, and stick to the time you have set. Don't forget to plan a treat to reward yourself for all your hard work after completing your task!

I'm finding it all too difficult – what shall I do?

At times you may feel that the E/RP exercise you have set is too difficult. If this occurs towards the start of your self-treatment, consider tackling a different task lower down on your OCD ladder. It does not matter if the task is too easy, because this will only give you confidence in your ability to face your fears and watch your anxiety lessen.

If you have completed all of the easier tasks on your ladder, tackle the more difficult E/RP exercises by breaking the problem down into manageable chunks. To remind yourself how to do this, look back at Chapter 9, 'Designing Exposure and Response Prevention Exercises'.

My anxiety ratings don't come down – why?

One of the main reasons for this is that your exposure is too short. It is important to allow yourself plenty of time to complete your E/RP exercises, and to keep doing them until your anxiety decreases. This could take up to two hours on your first trial, but will gradually get easier (and quicker) the more you practise.

You may like to get one of your parents or another person to assist you in judging when you should finish your E/RP task. A rule of thumb is to stop when your rating drops to a minimum of 2, but if possible keep going until your fear rating is 0.

Making an OCD timetable

Use this timetable to plan your OCD exercises. Don't forget to plan some rewards for yourself after all of your hard work!

	Monday	Tuesday	Wednesday	Thursday	Friday	Saturday	Sunday
8:00							
9:00							
10:00							
11:00							
12:00							
1:00							

	Monday	Tuesday	Wednesday	Thursday	Friday	Saturday	Sunday
2:00							
3:00							
4:00							
5:00							
6:00							
7:00							
8:00							

Another reason why your anxiety rating may not come down is that you could be doing *another* compulsion that you weren't fully aware of. For example, if you are doing an exposure task to germs on your hands, and you are deliberately not washing your hands so that you can learn to tolerate the anxiety that occurs, then this task should work to decrease your anxiety over time. However, if you are telling yourself that germs on your hands don't live for more that two hours anyway, then this is a type of *reassurance*, which is another compulsion, and your anxiety may not come down because you are not properly facing the fear of having germs on your hands.

It is very important to stop *all* compulsions when doing an exposure task, and this includes reassuring yourself or asking others for reassurance. You will need to be firm with yourself and resist any need to seek reassurance or engage in rituals if you want to overcome your OCD. If you do accidentally use a compulsion to help you feel better, stop and restart the E/RP exercise without the ritual.

I keep avoiding things – is this OK?

When you are doing your E/RP exercises it is important not to avoid touching things or avoid doing certain activities. If you do this, it will only maintain your difficulties with OCD and make your problems continue. When you design your E/RP exercises make sure that you list the problems that could get in the way, and get one of your parents or a helper to remind you to use this list to check that you are not avoiding anything.

I'm doing a few hidden compulsions – what should I do?

Hidden compulsions (also called 'covert compulsions') are just compulsions that you carry out in your head. These may be repeating phrases or numbers inside your head, praying, or imagining scenes to yourself, all of which are attempts at reducing your worry. Sometimes individuals with OCD stop engaging in obvious compulsions that can be seen by others, and instead replace these with more hidden or covert mental rituals. You will need to conduct your E/RP exercises without doing these covert compulsions.

What can I do if new compulsions arise?

This is common. You may find that once you have overcome one ritual, a new one emerges to replace it. It is therefore important to keep your OCD ladder up to date, so that you can target new compulsions with E/RP as they crop up. It is important to catch new compulsions early, before they become too established and are more difficult to change.

My thoughts are too worrying – how can I tackle these?

For some people with OCD, their thoughts and beliefs about what will occur if they do not engage in their compulsions are very strong and upsetting.

With OCD, it is common to have thoughts about something unpleasant happening to yourself or others, or a belief that you are responsible for preventing bad things from happening. For example, Lucy believed that unless she checked all of the windows and doors, the house would definitely be burgled. However, if these thoughts and beliefs are so strong that they prevent you from making any changes through doing E/RP exercises, you will need to take a slightly different approach as outlined in the following two chapters.

Most people find that resisting carrying out compulsions through doing E/RP exercises makes the thoughts much weaker, and that eventually they go away on their own. If you find that doing E/RP exercises is not really getting to your true thoughts, then it is also important that you read the next two chapters.

LEON

Leon developed an obsessional thought that if he did not complete his checking rituals at home then something awful would happen to his family, and it would be completely his fault. In his mind he saw images of his family members horrifically injured. He believed that checking light switches, the door handles and window locks prevented an intruder from entering the home and murdering his family. If any family member went out of the house, he would ask them repeatedly for reassurance that they were going to return, and he would need them to say over and over again 'I'll be back safe and soon.' All family members were requested to ring Leon at home every half-hour, to provide him with reassurance that they were OK. In each phone call they needed to repeat 'I'll be back safe and soon.' Leon tried to target these problems through E/RP exercises but quickly found himself avoiding making any changes. He used a timetable to schedule in his E/RP tasks, but never stuck to his plans. When he conducted his E/RP exercises he introduced further rituals in order to try to prevent awful things happening, and was unwilling to attempt E/RP without some form of compulsions.

Leon found that he was becoming more and more unmotivated to change his OCD through E/RP. He never learned that his anxiety levels would naturally decrease if he did not engage in compulsions. He was very concerned that if he did not engage in his compulsions, something truly horrible would happen to his family, and it would be his fault. This was not a risk he was willing to take. He needed to try different exercises that also targeted his thoughts, as these were getting in the way of him allowing himself to make progress. One way of fighting OCD thoughts uses *behavioural experiments*, and you can learn more about them in the next chapter.

WHAT SHOULD I DO NEXT?

If you have problems making progress with your E/RP exercises, there may be several reasons for this. Use Worksheet 11.2 to help you understand your difficulties and plan your next move against OCD.

How to understand difficulties with E/RP exercises

These questions can help you to think about the problems you may be having with your E/RP exercises, and will guide you towards solving the problems.

Do you ever think about doing your E/RP exercises but do not get around to them? What stops you from doing them?

Do your anxiety ratings drop when you engage in E/RP exercises?

Did you do anything to reduce your anxiety during the task? If so, what was it?

Did you do any hidden ritual inside your head during your task (e.g. counting, praying, repeating phrases, reassuring yourself that everything would be OK)? What was the ritual?

Are you avoiding anything after doing your E/RP exercise? If so, what?

What are your obsessional thoughts?

Are these thoughts so upsetting that you are finding it impossible to risk changing any compulsions through E/RP exercises?

What do you need to do to overcome your difficulty?

What will be your plan of action?

SUMMARY

- It is normal for problems to arise when conducting your E/RP exercises.

- Use Worksheet 11.2 to help you identify any behaviours that could be stopping you overcoming your difficulties with OCD.

- Make a plan to tackle any problems that arise.

- If you are having very strong obsessional thoughts, and are not making progress, carefully read through the next few chapters.

Now turn to the next chapter on page 132

ADVICE FOR PARENTS OR CARERS

Your child's progress and motivation to engage in E/RP exercises may be influenced by their fear of disappointing others, fear of failure, or fear of pressure. Sometimes your child may also be a perfectionist, so even small changes are perceived as not 'good enough'. This may lead to your child being excessively self-critical, and unwilling to risk engaging in treatment.

As OCD is likely to have been a cause of upset for all family members, it is understandable that any sign of improvement can lead to increased demands from family members to stop engaging in compulsions. OCD is likely to be impacting on family relationships and possibly educational achievement. Family members wanting their child to be free from OCD can lead to them trying to rush their child, or can lead to unintended pressure. It is important to be patient, and not to push for change faster than your child can manage. Remember to use the OCD ladder to remind yourself of what E/RP tasks are manageable and what E/RP tasks are currently out of your child's reach.

TYLER

Tyler, aged 12 years, refused to engage in any E/RP tasks for his OCD at home. He found it difficult initially to pick someone to help and virtually impossible to discuss his OCD openly with his family. He did, however, privately attempt E/RP exercises when at school, but never shared any progress with anyone. He found it hard to make friends as he was very sensitive to what he believed others were thinking about him. Tyler was worried that if he started to show any signs of improvement, then others' expectations that he should conquer his OCD would be overwhelming. He was very sensitive to feeling pressured to make progress, and feared risking failure and disappointing others.

SUMMARY

- Fear of pressure, failure or disappointing others may lead your child to avoid engaging in E/RP tasks.

- Remember to progress at your child's pace.

- Be patient and use the OCD ladder for guidance.

Chapter 12   # What is the Role of My Thoughts?

People with OCD have thoughts that are distressing. This chapter aims to help you to understand the role of your thoughts. It also explores how to identify the OCD thoughts that you have, and how to challenge such unhelpful thoughts with more helpful ones.

HOW IMPORTANT ARE YOUR THOUGHTS?

Everyone has thoughts or images that run through their head. Often these are pleasant or neutral thoughts, about friends, things they are going to do, or what might be happening. At other times the thoughts can be unpleasant and distressing. These are called *intrusive thoughts*.

Sometimes the intrusive thoughts can be very upsetting, such as worries about something bad happening to yourself or to people that you love. For example, if a parent or carer is late home from work, you might start to worry that they have had a terrible accident. It is normal to have thoughts like this occasionally, almost everyone does. However, if you have OCD, these intrusive thoughts tend to stay in your mind for a long time, or they keep coming back into your mind over and over again – and when they do you naturally feel worried or upset by them. OCD convinces you that you have to do certain compulsions or avoid certain situations in order to prevent these upsetting thoughts from coming true. In short, *OCD is tricking you*.

Sometimes, in order to stop these upsetting thoughts from coming back, it's enough to just recognize that the thoughts are OCD thoughts, but you can *ignore them* and carry on doing whatever you should be doing. Some people find it easier than others to just ignore thoughts. If you don't find it very easy to ignore OCD thoughts, then there are some other ideas that might help you later in this chapter and in the next two chapters.

WHAT ARE TYPICAL OCD THOUGHTS?

People with OCD are more likely to have certain types of thoughts, compared to people without OCD. Read the sections below and see if any of these types of OCD thoughts are similar to the thoughts you experience. Then continue reading the chapter to learn how to challenge these ways of thinking.

Thinking you are responsible when you are not

Do you feel too responsible for preventing bad things from happening to yourself or to others? If so, many of your compulsions may be aimed at preventing harmful events from occurring. For example, Kyle repeatedly checked that all the windows and doors were locked, as he felt responsible for preventing a burglary. His OCD had *tricked him* into believing that he was responsible for preventing bad things from happening.

Magical thinking

Do you have magical or extremely superstitious thoughts? Do you believe that your thoughts are so important that having a bad or horrible thought will definitely lead to a bad event occurring? For example, Jade believed that if she did not avoid certain numbers that she thought were unlucky (i.e. 6, 13, 66, 666), then something bad would happen to a member of her family. Her OCD had *tricked her* into believing that her thoughts had a magical ability to control things that happened to her and to others.

Over-importance of thoughts

Do you believe that all of your intrusive thoughts are extremely important and that you need to respond to them? Do you also believe that having such thoughts means that you are a bad, crazy or dangerous person? For example, Justin believed that if he had a bad thought about pushing someone down the stairs, it meant that he would actually push someone down the stairs unless he did a compulsion to prevent this. His compulsions were all aimed at ensuring that he didn't harm anyone. He believed his thoughts and believed that OCD was protecting him from doing something to harm others and thus become a murderer. His OCD had *tricked him* into believing that his intrusive thoughts were all-important.

Liking to be certain

Do you need to feel 100 per cent certain about everything? Do you need to know for certain that bad things will not happen? For example, Sonia was so anxious about not being able to cope with bad things happening in her life that she constantly asked for reassurance from her parents that bad things would not happen. Although her parents' reassurance made her feel better in the short term, she never learned that things could not be 100 per cent controlled. This is a common way of thinking by individuals with OCD. Her OCD had *tricked her* into thinking that she could control everything, and that reassurance would prevent something upsetting from happening.

Liking to be perfect

Do you spend a long time trying to get things absolutely right? Do you need to feel that things are 'just right', and if they aren't then it feels intolerable? Do you try to control events in your life by doing things 100 per cent perfectly? If you do not feel like you have done things perfectly, do you then feel like a failure? For example, Ellie felt that she had to check her written work over and over in case she had inadvertently made a mistake or written a rude word. It would take hours just to complete a paragraph that she felt did not contain any such words or errors. Her OCD had *tricked her* into believing that she needed to do things perfectly to feel in control.

In order to really understand your thoughts, it would be helpful now complete Worksheet 12.1.

✓

How to understand my thoughts

Complete the following sentences to understand how OCD tricks you.

My OCD is triggered when:

My OCD makes me worry that:

It also makes me worry that:

Tick which of the following OCD thoughts you also have, and give an example of how OCD tricks you in the space provided.

❑   Feeling too responsible

My OCD tricks me into thinking that:

❑   Magical thinking

My OCD tricks me into thinking that:

✓

❑   Over-importance of thoughts

My OCD tricks me into thinking that:

❑   Liking to be certain

My OCD tricks me into thinking that:

❑   Liking to be perfect

My OCD tricks me into thinking that:

THINKING HELPFUL THOUGHTS

As you have just read, OCD plays tricks on your thoughts by making you think in unhelpful ways. For example, if you have fears about germs and you catch a cold, OCD will trick you into thinking that this is your fault for not doing your OCD compulsions correctly. This is an unhelpful thought. If you have OCD you have probably forgotten that you do have a choice in how you think about things, and it has probably become quite difficult for you to think in more helpful ways.

In order to recover from OCD, you will need to practise helpful thoughts or thoughts that challenge your OCD. A more helpful thought for the above example might be 'I caught a cold as my best friend also has a cold, and I'm not going to let OCD trick me into thinking that it is my fault.' You can practise understanding your unhelpful and helpful thoughts by completing Worksheet 12.2.

✓

Having helpful thoughts

Try to think about some things that have happened to you recently. Then think of some helpful and unhelpful thoughts for each of these things. We've given you an example.

What happened?
My friend was 30 minutes late to meet me and we missed the movie that we wanted to see.

My unhelpful thoughts were:
She did that deliberately because she didn't want to see the movie I had picked.

My helpful thoughts were:
She got stuck on a slow bus and couldn't get here any earlier. At least we got to spend some time together and we can always go and see the movie another time.

What happened?

My unhelpful thoughts were:

My helpful thoughts were:

What happened?

My unhelpful thoughts were:

My helpful thoughts were:

WHAT TO SAY TO OCD

You need to let OCD know that you are in charge. One way of doing this is to talk back to your OCD and to tell it that you are not going to be pushed around. For example, you might say to your OCD:

I know you are trying to trick me into feeling scared; you are trying to be in control of my thoughts. I am not going to listen to you or do what you ask. I am the one that will be in control of my thoughts!

Now it's your turn. Can you think of four or five statements that will let OCD know that you are the one who is in charge? Remember that you can choose to let OCD know that you are just going to ignore the thoughts and wait for them to go away. Try to make your statements back to the OCD really strong messages.

1. ....
   ....

2. ....
   ....

3. ....
   ....

4. ....

....

5. ....

....

HOW TO THINK HELPFUL THOUGHTS

If you now recognize that OCD is tricking you into thinking in a certain way, then read the following sections to get an idea of some helpful thoughts that you could practise. Add any helpful thoughts of your own in the spaces provided.

Helpful thoughts against feeling too responsible

If you have strong thoughts about being responsible for preventing bad events from happening, then try practising the following helpful ways of thinking:

- OCD is tricking me into feeling responsible for events that I have no control over; I am not going to let it.

- If something bad happens it is not my fault.

- Other people don't have to complete compulsions to stop bad things from happening.

- There many reasons for bad things happening, none of which are related to me or to my OCD.

- Or I could say:

....

....

Helpful thoughts against magical thinking

If you have magical or extremely superstitious thoughts, then try practising the following helpful ways of thinking:

- OCD is tricking me into thinking that my thoughts have magical abilities; they don't.

- I cannot control events just by thinking about them.

- I think that certain letters, numbers or objects are unlucky, but this is just unhelpful magical thinking; there is no evidence that they are.

- Or I could say:

....

....

Helpful thoughts against the over-importance of thoughts

If you have thoughts that seem too important and distressing, then try practising the following helpful ways of thinking:

- This is only an intrusive thought; if I ignore it then it will eventually stop upsetting me.

- Intrusive thoughts are normal, almost everybody gets them, and it doesn't mean anything.

- Just because I have a thought about doing something horrible does not mean that I would actually do it.

- Or I could say:

....

....

Helpful thoughts against liking to be certain

If you have thoughts that you need to feel 100 per cent certain about events, and you frequently ask for reassurance from others, then try practising the following helpful ways of thinking:

- OCD is tricking me; I can't be certain about everything.

- OCD compulsions do not guarantee that bad things will not happen, they just guarantee that I will stay feeling miserable.

- I need to practise feeling OK about not always knowing what will happen.

- Life is uncertain, and I can cope with anything it throws at me without my OCD.

- Or I could say:

....

....

Helpful thoughts against liking to be perfect

If you have thoughts that you need to do things 100 per cent perfectly, then try practising the following helpful ways of thinking:

- No one can do everything perfectly all of the time.

- I need to do things to a good enough level, not perfectly.

- It's OK to make mistakes; no one is 100 per cent perfect.

- Or I could say:

....

....

Now use Worksheet 12.3 to help you to challenge your unhelpful OCD thoughts with more helpful ones.

Thinking more helpful OCD thoughts

Think about your OCD thoughts. What unhelpful thoughts does OCD make you have? What helpful thoughts can you use instead? Answer these questions to help you get control back over your OCD thoughts.

What might trigger your OCD?

My unhelpful OCD thoughts are:

My helpful OCD thoughts are:

MORE ABOUT FIGHTING BACK WITH HELPFUL THOUGHTS

Sometimes your OCD will trick you into believing that it is just too difficult to overcome your problems. Then you will need to practise fighting back. Below is a list of fighting thoughts that might help you when you are finding things a little difficult. Remember to tell yourself these thoughts frequently as this will help you to feel more confident and help you progress and get OCD out of your life. If you can think of any other helpful fighting thoughts, add these to the end of the list.

- Fighting OCD will be hard, but I know that I can do it.

- I will try my hardest, and if I keep practising it will get easier.

- I have beaten OCD before, and I can do it again.

- This task is tough, but I know that it is just an OCD worry.

- This is just my anxiety being set off at the wrong time.

- I know that I have succeeded in tasks so far and nothing bad has happened.

- What would a friend who doesn't have OCD do in this situation?

- Experiencing anxiety during my E/RP task is a good thing. I know that it will reduce and this means that my tasks will help me to get rid of OCD.

- If I feel an urge to avoid my anxiety, I can gain control by doing the opposite of what OCD would want me to do.

- Letting thoughts pass without acting on them weakens their strength. The more that I practise, the easier it becomes.

- Get lost OCD! I don't want you in my life anymore.

- Or I could say:

....

....

....

....

WHAT SHOULD I DO NEXT?

You have now started to understand what is in your thoughts, and to challenge your unhelpful thoughts with more helpful ones. You will need this information for the next two chapters, where you will learn more skills to help you overcome OCD. Look back over your earlier worksheets and write down here the OCD thoughts and beliefs that you now need to change.

My unhelpful OCD thoughts that I need to change are:

1. ....
....

2. ....
....

3. ....
....

SUMMARY

- Intrusive thoughts are normal. Almost everyone has them some of the time.

- OCD thoughts tend to follow certain patterns.

- You can challenge OCD thoughts by thinking more helpful thoughts.

- Make an action plan of what OCD thoughts you need to work on.

Now turn to the next chapter on page 147

ADVICE FOR PARENTS OR CARERS

This chapter aims to teach your child how to identify the OCD thoughts that they experience. There are unhelpful ways of thinking about things that are typical of OCD. The most typical thinking style is believing that you can prevent bad things from occurring by engaging in OCD compulsions. This is called 'inflated responsibility'. Other typical thoughts include magical thinking, over-importance of thoughts, intolerance of uncertainty, and perfectionism. These ways of thinking are described earlier in this chapter.

It is also common that young people with OCD can have really distressing thoughts or images that have a violent or sexual content. Remind yourself and your child that although these thoughts are distressing they are just intrusive thoughts. They do not reflect his or her wishes or desires. They do not mean that your child is going to act on any of these thoughts. In fact, having these sorts of thoughts is extremely distressing and upsetting for your child, and it is important that you can remind them that the thoughts do not reflect on them in any way.

If your child has lots of upsetting obsessional thoughts it is important that they start to build their skills in thought challenging. This is essentially a form of 'talking back' to their OCD by using more helpful thoughts. The chapter contains examples of helpful thoughts that your child could use for talking back to the various OCD intrusive thoughts, but your child may need to adapt these to their unique obsessions. You may have a role in helping them generate alternative helpful thoughts, and to remind them to practise these thoughts when they are particularly worried. This is a useful skill to develop, and is helpful if your child is so distressed by their obsessional thoughts that they are not progressing with their E/RP exercises.

SUMMARY

- Inflated responsibility is a common thinking style in OCD.

- Obsessional thoughts can be violent or sexual in nature.

- Obsessional thoughts do not reflect your child's wishes or desires, and they do not mean that he or she is going to act on the thoughts. The opposite is true. These thoughts cause a great deal of distress and upset.

- Thought challenging can be helpful for overcoming obsessional thoughts.

Chapter 13

How Can I Challenge My Thoughts?

In the previous chapter you learned how to challenge your OCD thinking by responding to your unhelpful thoughts with more helpful ways of thinking. In this chapter you will learn two more techniques that could be useful in helping you challenge your OCD thoughts: 'putting your OCD on trial', and the 'responsibility pie-chart'.

LEARNING TO PUT OCD WORRIES ON TRIAL

OCD tries to convince you that your thoughts are too important and will come true if you do not complete your compulsions. 'Putting your thoughts on trial' is a technique that helps you see that there is no evidence for the things that OCD is making you believe. For this

technique to work, you will need to act as if you are a judge and to look for evidence that your OCD thoughts are actually true. This is sometimes called the 'Theory A or Theory B' technique. Image that 'Theory A' is your OCD worry, whereas 'Theory B' is a possible alternative explanation. Essentially you will learn to gather evidence to see which theory fits the facts. This probably sounds complicated, so let's see how it works in practice by looking at how Jayne used the 'thoughts on trial' technique to challenge her thoughts.

JAYNE

Jayne worried that having an intrusive thought about a poor person would also make her poor in the future. To prevent this she would imagine a rich person instead. Jayne rated the strength of her belief that she would become poor without her compulsion as 85 per cent. She predicted her anxiety at resisting the compulsion as 7 out of 10 on her OCD ladder. Because of this she decided to put her thoughts on trial. She had these two different theories:

Theory A (OCD theory)	Theory B (alternative theory)
I will become poor if I don't cancel out my thoughts	I cannot control future events with my thoughts

Jayne thought about the evidence that she had for both of her theories and listed them, as you will see in Figure 12.

Theory A	Theory B
I will become poor if I don't cancel out my thoughts	I cannot control future events with my thoughts
So far I haven't become poor, but is this because of my compulsion?	Having a picture of a rich person in my head doesn't make me wealthy.
I haven't heard of anyone being able to control events with their thoughts before.	My friends and family don't have to do this behaviour to stop themselves from becoming poor, why would it be any different for me?
How could this be scientifically possible?	I know that I have OCD; this is just another OCD worry.
	I have resisted OCD compulsions in the past and nothing bad has happened.
	OCD is just a problem with anxiety, and I have learnt that anxiety reduces over time.
Belief rating: 45%	Belief rating: 55%

Figure 12 Jayne's 'thoughts on trial' chart

After putting her thoughts and beliefs on trial, Jayne realized that she had more evidence that she could *not* control future events with her thoughts. She was then ready to test out her thoughts using behavioural experiments. You can learn more about these in the next chapter.

Now it is time to put your own thoughts on trial. Complete Worksheet 13.1 to see how your thoughts stand up to the evidence!

How to put my thoughts on trial

First write down your OCD worry. Call this 'Theory A'.

How much do you believe Theory A is true? Score it from 0 to 100.

Now write down an alternative explanation. Call this 'Theory B'.

How much do you believe Theory B is true? Score it from 0 to 100.

Next, complete the chart on the next page with evidence for and against each theory. Useful questions to ask yourself are:

- What has happened in the past?
- What is more likely to happen?
- What has happened to other people?
- How would this be possible?

Write evidence for Theory A here	Write evidence for Theory B here
Belief rating: %	Belief rating: %

- Write down how much you *now* believe your Theory A is true (0–100).

- Write down how much you *now* believe Theory B is true (0–100).

- What is your next step in overcoming OCD? Write it out below:

HOW TO MAKE A RESPONSIBILITY PIE-CHART

You may have seen the words 'responsibility pie-chart' and immediately thought that we are going to have a maths lesson. Of course we are not! This is just a helpful drawing technique to use when you have lots of worries about feeling responsible for bad things happening.

Instead of listening to your OCD, which is telling you that you are 100 per cent responsible for bad events occurring, the responsibility pie-chart technique helps you to look at your fears in a more careful and reasonable way. It helps you to think about your worry in the same way that a person who does not have OCD would think about it. It will also help you reassess how responsible you actually are, and the many other reasons that could contribute to something unfortunate happening.

The example of Justin will help you understand how to use the pie-chart technique. After you have read this, use Worksheet 13.2 to start to change your feelings of responsibility.

JUSTIN

Justin believed that if he did not wash his hands four times after he touched something he thought had germs on it, then his mum or dad would become sick. He believed that he would be 100 per cent responsible if his parents did get ill. He completed the responsibility pie-chart to think about his fears. First he made a list of all the possible reasons that could lead to his parents getting sick. He needed to discuss this with his dad because to start with he could not think of any reason, except himself, that could cause the event to happen. He then gave each reason on the list a percentage score of how likely a cause it might be of his parents' sickness (see Figure 13). This needed to add up to 100 per cent. He then plotted this on a pie-chart (see Figure 14). From looking at his pie-chart he realized that there are many reasons that his parents might get ill, and none of them were his fault. He found out that OCD was making him feel 100 per cent responsible for events when he was *not* responsible at all.

Possible cause of mum or dad getting sick	How much do I believe this could cause my parents illness (as a percentage)?
Caught an illness from someone at work	28%
Ate something bad	27%
Being stressed and run down	22%
Got caught out in the rain and wind without a coat	10%
Got an allergy, such as hay fever	13%
Me not washing my hands	0%

Figure 13 Justin's responsibility pie-chart ratings

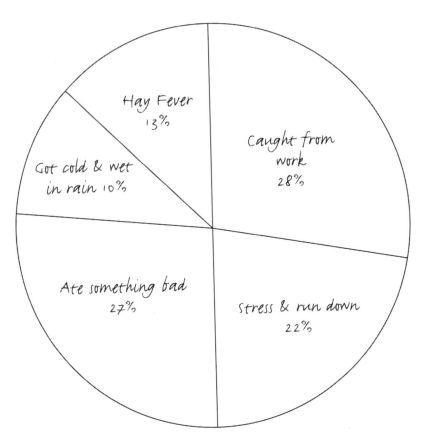

Figure 14 Justin's pie-chart

Now use Worksheet 13.2 to work on changing your feelings of responsibility.

How to make my own responsibility pie-chart

What awful thing does OCD tell you that you will be responsible for?

How much do you think you would be responsible, on a 0–100 per cent scale, if this actually happened?

List below all the other possible reasons that might account for this happening, and give each a percentage (to add up to a total of 100). Figure 13 showed you how Justin did this. Place the score for your role at the bottom of the box.

All of the possible causes of the awful thing happening	How much do I believe this could be the cause (as a percentage)?
	%
	%
	%
	%
	%
	%
	%
	%
My role	%

Draw your pie-chart

Divide up your pie-chart below into slices (called segments) to roughly show the reasons for your feared event happening. You could start with your own role's score. Label the slices.

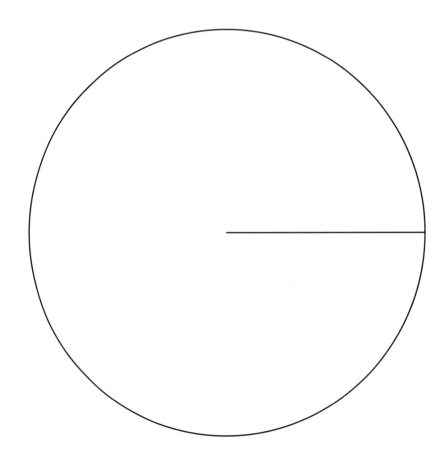

Look carefully at your responsibility pie-chart. Do you now think that you will definitely be responsible if the awful event occurs? Tick the box.

❏   Yes

❏   No

So now, how much would you think you were responsible, on a 0–100 per cent scale, if this actually happened?

...........%

WHAT SHOULD I DO NEXT?

Putting your thoughts on trial and the responsibility pie-chart are both really useful techniques to use if you hold strong OCD beliefs. From 'putting your thoughts on trial' you can start to build up evidence *against* your thoughts. From using the responsibility pie-chart technique you can learn that there are various reasons for bad events happening which are not related at all to your OCD.

When you have learned how to identify your OCD thoughts and start to challenge them, you will be ready to test your thoughts through what we call 'behavioural experiments'. You will learn how to go about this in the next chapter.

SUMMARY

- Challenge your OCD thoughts by putting your thoughts on trial.

- If you have upsetting thoughts that you are responsible for bad things happening, use the responsibility pie-chart technique.

- Remember to use these techniques if you are feeling out of control with your OCD thoughts.

Now turn to the next chapter on page 159

ADVICE FOR PARENTS OR CARERS

This chapter aims to teach two more skills that are useful if your child is having lots of distressing OCD thoughts: 'putting your thoughts on trial', and the 're-sponsibility pie-chart'. These are aimed at giving your child some additional skills they may need to challenge their OCD thoughts. You might have a role in helping them generate information to support a 'Theory B' in 'putting your thoughts on trial', or reasons for a feared event occurring in the responsibility pie-chart. Initially it can be difficult for your child to think of anything other than their OCD thoughts. With practice they will develop the skills to challenge their thoughts more independently.

WHEN OBSESSIONAL THOUGHTS INVOLVE YOU

You will need to be sensitive to the possibility that your child may not want to share obsessional thoughts or images with you. This could be related to their developmental need to be independent and organize their own self-treatment. However, occasionally their OCD beliefs may be about you. For example, Emma had obsessional thoughts that her parents would be horrifically murdered if she did not engage in various compulsions. She also believed that if she talked about these thoughts or images then OCD might punish her by making them come true.

Never force your adolescent to disclose the content of their obsessional thoughts. If your child is avoiding talking about their OCD beliefs due to fears that they will occur, these need to be added to their OCD ladder and tackled through E/RP tasks (e.g. finding little ways to gradually talk about the content of thoughts) or through behavioural experiments (see the following chapter).

SUMMARY

- Practise helping your child challenge his or her thoughts by using the techniques of 'thoughts on trial' and a 'responsibility pie-chart'.

- Be sensitive that the content of your child's thoughts may involve you.

- Tackle such thoughts through carefully planned E/RP exercises or through behavioural experiments.

Chapter 14

How Can I Test Whether My Thoughts Will Come True?

WHAT IS A BEHAVIOURAL EXPERIMENT?

In the previous chapters you learned that young people with OCD often have thoughts and beliefs about what will happen if they do not do their compulsions. If these beliefs are really strong (say you believe at least 70 per cent that they will come true), it can be difficult to ignore the thoughts and wait for them to go away.

How can you reduce the amount you believe the OCD thoughts to be true? One method is a *behavioural experiment*, which is aimed at helping you challenge your thinking. You will learn here how to conduct an 'experiment' to test your thoughts and beliefs.

WHY SHOULD I DO BEHAVIOURAL EXPERIMENTS?

If you are making good progress in overcoming OCD with E/RP exercises, then there may be no need to use other techniques to help. Instead, you might like to just continue working up your ladder using E/RP.

However, if you are finding that intrusive thoughts are still upsetting, then learning to conduct behavioural experiments may be helpful. This is because behavioural experiments target your thoughts and beliefs. They are particularly useful if you have very strong worries about the consequences of not doing compulsions.

ASHLEY

Ashley, aged 16 years, had obsessional thoughts about contamination. He cleaned or avoided anything that he saw as toxic or that he thought had been in contact with chemicals. His compulsions ranged from avoiding touching door handles, fuel and cleaning products, as well as excessive hand-washing. His belief was that if he had any contact with chemicals etc. they would enter his brain and lead to sickness, blindness or complete loss of control through madness. He was finding it difficult to drop all of his compulsions when doing his E/RP exercises. Even learning that his anxiety level would drop did not stop his worries about his health. He needed to practise behavioural experiments that were set up to test out whether his beliefs were true.

HOW DO BEHAVIOURAL EXPERIMENTS WORK?

Doing behavioural experiments is similar to doing E/RP exercises, but the two techniques work in different ways to weaken OCD.

- In E/RP exercises the aim is to learn gradually that you can cope with your feelings of anxiety without doing your compulsions.

- The aim of behavioural experiments is to learn that the feared consequence of not doing the ritual *does not in fact come true*.

HOW TO CARRY OUT A BEHAVIOURAL EXPERIMENT

You will still need to use your OCD ladder as described in Chapter 9, 'Designing Exposure and Response Prevention Exercises'. Now the goal is to use your ladder to conduct experiments that test your thoughts and beliefs. You will still need to do E/RP exercises as well, because using more than one method can help you to overcome your OCD more quickly. Worksheet 14.1 can be used to help you do your behavioural experiments.

Worksheet 14.1

My behavioural experiment

Day:					
OCD thought to be tested:					
How much do you believe that this thought is true (score 0–100):					
What to do to test my thought	Likely problems	How to deal with problems	Date of experiment	Outcome of experiment	Re-rate my belief in this thought

A step-by-step guide to completing your behavioural experiments

- Step 1. Pick an OCD difficulty from your ladder.

- Step 2. Think about what your worries are if you do not do your compulsion.

- Step 3. Write down the thought or belief that you want to test. Write this in the space provided on Worksheet 14.1. This thought then becomes a *prediction* that you can put to the test by doing an experiment.

- Step 4. Using a 0–100 per cent scale, rate how much you think this belief is true. Remember that 0 means 'I do not believe that this thought is true at all', and 100 per cent means 'I am completely convinced that this thought is true'. Write this down on Worksheet 14.1.

- Step 5. Write down what you plan to do to test your thoughts.

- Step 6. To increase your chances of success, think about any likely problems that you might encounter. Write these on the worksheet.

- Step 7. Write down how you plan to overcome these problems.

- Step 8. Plan a date to complete your experiment.

- Step 9. Carry out the behavioural experiment.

- Step 10. Write down the outcome of your experiment.

- Step 11. Re-rate how much you now think your original belief is true.

<hr>

ASHLEY

Ashley developed an OCD ladder to use in his E/RP tasks and behavioural experiments. Towards the bottom of his ladder he had written the difficulty 'avoiding touching washing powder'. He believed that if he touched the washing powder without washing his hands then he would get sick. He rated his belief that this thought would come true as 50 per cent. By doing his behavioural experiment he was trying to find out whether he really would get sick if he touched the powder. He found out that his fears did *not* come true – he did not get sick by touching washing powder. He now rated his belief in the thought 'I will get sick if I touch washing powder' as down to 10 per cent. This rating dropped to 0 when he repeated this experiment several times, as he found out for himself that touching washing powder never led to illness. He conducted behavioural experiments in this way for some of the other items on his OCD ladder.

<hr>

Figure 15 gives you details of Ashley's behavioural experiment. You can use this as a guide to complete your own worksheet.

HOW TO OVERCOME PROBLEMS WITH BEHAVIOURAL EXPERIMENTS

As you work through your ladder, conducting behavioural experiments, you can look back at Chapter 11, 'Overcoming Difficulties', to get some ideas. The sections below explain some difficulties that often arise when people conduct behavioural experiments.

It's too risky – I'm too afraid to change anything as something bad might happen

At first it may be difficult to risk conducting a behavioural experiment as you may worry that your fears will come true. This is a normal worry. OCD has probably been controlling your thoughts and behaviour for a long time. However, the more you do E/RP exercises and behavioural experi-

Day: Wednesday				
OCD thought to be tested: If I touch the washing powder box and do not wash my hands, I will get sick				
How much do you believe that this thought is true (score 0–100): 50%				
What to do to test my thought	Likely problems	How to deal with problems	Outcome of experiment	Re-rate my belief in this thought
Touch the washing powder box, and do not wash my hands for 1 hr	1. Avoid doing it 2. Avoid touching anything for 1 hr 3. Get angry	1. Agree with mum a plan, stick to it 2. Touch items such as TV 3. Challenge angry thoughts, and do an activity to calm down	Completed experiment twice. Did not wash hands, did not get angry. Was able to touch objects and even ate my lunch!	10%

Figure 15 Ashley's first behavioural experiment result

ments, the sooner you will start to realize that OCD *is not telling you the truth*. Remind yourself that you cannot control events in your world just by thinking, or by doing things the way OCD would like you to do them. Bad things do not occur just because you have not completed your compulsions! If you are having trouble getting started, look back over Chapter 12 to remind yourself of some tools that you could use to challenge your OCD thinking.

I've been practising behavioural experiments, but my beliefs don't seem to change

Check that you have not introduced another compulsion or avoidance behaviour when conducting your behavioural experiment. If you have, this will stop you finding out that your fears do not come true when you drop your rituals. Re-run the experiment without your extra avoidance behaviours or compulsions. Use your helper and Worksheet 14.1 to plan how to do this.

What if my fears do come true?

Sometimes bad things can happen in life. It is a coincidence that they happen while you are practising your behavioural experiments. For example, if you have contamination fears, it is possible that you may catch an illness at some point during your self-treatment for your OCD. It is important to think about *why* you might have got sick. You could use a responsibility pie-chart to help you do this. Getting sick occurs for many reasons, and everyone gets ill at some point. Your OCD will try to convince you that you could have prevented this by engaging in compulsions. *Don't believe it*. Re-read Chapter 13, 'How Can I Challenge My Thoughts?', and keep challenging your OCD thoughts. Lessen their hold on you by continuing to practise E/RP exercises and behavioural experiments.

ASHLEY

Ashley gradually worked through his OCD ladder to tackle more difficult items at the top. An experiment towards the top of the ladder was to 'touch the front door handle without tissue paper on a day that his father had put petrol in his lawn mower'. This was an important experiment as he believed that getting petrol into his eyes would lead him to become blind. He had a 90 per cent belief that this would come true. Ashley ran into difficulties with the experiment. Although he did not use tissue paper to open the door, he used his sleeve instead, and then avoided touching anything until he could wash his hands and change his shirt. His beliefs did not change, as he did not properly test out whether touching the door handle would lead to going blind. He needed to repeat the experiment, dropping all of his old and new compulsions and facing his fears. When he did this he realized that touching the door was not dangerous, and it was then that his belief in the OCD worry dropped.

Ashley's behavioural experiment is shown in Figure 16.

Day: **Saturday**					
OCD thought to be tested: If I touch the front door without tissue paper on a day when dad mows the lawn, petrol will get into my eyes and I will go blind					
How much do you believe that this thought is true (score 0–100): **90%**					
What to do to test my thought	Likely problems	How to deal with problems	Outcome of experiment	Re-rate my belief in this thought	
Touch the front door without tissue paper, and do not wash my hands for 1 hr	1. Avoid the most risky days, such as when dad has used the lawn mower so that there is petrol on it. 2. Avoid touching anything for 1 hr	1. Do it on a day that dad is gardening 2. Touch items in bedroom after touching the front door without tissue paper	Avoided doing task by covering my hands in my sleeves, stayed away from touching anything after touching the front door.	90%	

Figure 16 Ashley's second behavioural experiment result

WHAT SHOULD I DO NEXT?

Spend time thinking about what you have learned when you complete each behavioural experiment. Use the *evidence* from your completed experiments to challenge your beliefs about your OCD. The more you do this, the quicker you will recover from OCD. Use Worksheet 14.2 to help you think about the results of your behavioural experiments, and to plan what to do next.

How to make sense of my behavioural experiment

Ask yourself these questions each time you have completed a behavioural experiment. This will help you understand what you have done and what this tells you about OCD. Jot down your answers here.

1. What was your experiment? What did you do?

2. What went well?

3. What did not go so well?

4. What did you think would happen?

5. What actually happened?

6. What have you learned from doing this experiment?

7. How does this help you change your beliefs about OCD?

8. Could you apply this information to other situations where OCD frightens you?

9. What do you need to do next? What are your new goals?

10. What difficulties might come up? How can you overcome them?

CHECK YOUR PROGRESS

The final chapter in this section looks at how to maintain the gains that you have made. Before you start to work through that chapter, it might be helpful to check on your progress so far. You can re-do the questionnaire in the Appendix of this book. You completed the questionnaire once before you started working through the chapters in Part B of this book, and on page 64 we suggested that you make a note of your scores. Do the questionnaire again now, and then add up the numbers in the same way that you did before. Put your scores in the space below.

Compulsions interference score:
Obsessions interference score:
TOTAL interference score:

Have your scores changed? If your scores have gone down, this suggests that you have been successful in fighting back against your OCD, and the OCD is now causing less trouble in your life than it did previously. If your scores have increased, or if your total score at this stage is 12 or more, it may be helpful for you to speak to your doctor about OCD, and he or she may suggest that you see a clinical psychologist or a psychiatrist who may be able to help you further.

SUMMARY

- Behavioural experiments help you challenge OCD thoughts.

- Use your OCD ladder to help you design experiments at different levels of difficulty.

- Complete behavioural experiments regularly (every day if possible).

- After your experiments, think about what you have learned about OCD.

- Notice your beliefs changing.

- Measure change using the questionnaire in the Appendix.

Now turn to the next chapter on page 173

ADVICE FOR PARENTS OR CARERS

This chapter outlines experiments that focus on the intrusive thoughts that your child experiences. The rationale for behavioural experiments is to challenge your child's specific beliefs and predictions about their OCD. This will involve your child taking a perceived risk, which initially will be very frightening. You will need to be supportive, but as always do not offer to do the compulsions for your child, and be sensitive to any of their attempts to avoid items or situations.

HOW TO HELP YOUR CHILD UNDERSTAND HIS OR HER BELIEFS

Young people may need help identifying their specific beliefs and predictions about OCD. If your child is struggling to identify these you could try asking 'So what is so bad (upsetting) about that?' By asking this question several times over, you may be able to help your child understand what their fears really are, and design experiments to test them out. The case below gives an illustration of this.

ASHLEY

Ashley and his school counsellor were finding it difficult to understand his fears about contamination. The counsellor asked him to think about why it would be so bad if the fears were true. Below is an example of their conversation.

Counsellor: Can you tell me why you are frightened of touching the door handle?

Ashley: It's contaminated... I'll get something off it.

Counsellor: So what would be so bad about getting something off it?

Ashley: It'll get inside my mouth.

Counsellor: So what would be so bad about that?

Ashley: It'll poison my insides and get into my brain.

Counsellor: So what would be so bad about it getting into your
          brain?

Ashley: I won't be able to think properly.

Counsellor: And what would be so bad about that?

Ashley: I would be completely out of control.

From the example it is clear that Ashley's real fears centre around
the belief that contact with chemicals, petrol and toxins could
lead to a loss of his ability to control his mind.

Experiments can then be designed to test out whether contact with feared sub-
stances (e.g. petrol) do lead to Ashley's feared outcomes coming true. It is essential to use the information gathered from such behavioural experiments to help
your child challenge their OCD beliefs.

SUMMARY

- Asking your child to think about what might happen if their fears did
  come true can help you and them to better understand what is
  underlying their OCD.

- Design behavioural experiments that are targeted at challenging your
  child's OCD thoughts.

- Offer to help them review their progress.

- Target any OCD predictions that involve yourself with behavioural
  experiments.

Chapter 15

How to Maintain the Gains I Have Made

The first thing to say is 'well done' for getting through the book this far! By now, you will have learned a lot about OCD, and a lot about how to beat your own OCD. Your life might have changed a lot as a result, or perhaps only a little bit. But the thing to think about now is where do you go from here? It is important to think about some of the ways in which you can stay on top of the OCD and maintain the gains you have made. Why is this important? The main reason is because OCD can be very unpredictable, and it can sometimes try to sneak back into your life and cause you as much trouble again. Health professionals might call this a 'setback' or a 'relapse'.

A setback is not unusual. In fact, most young people who have successfully beaten their OCD will find that they have to be very aware of OCD trying to come back. This is a normal part of what you can expect from OCD. We don't know why it does this; but if you are prepared for it, then it's not likely to shock you or upset you if it does happen.

The other thing to know is that, if OCD does try to come back, it is not likely to be as difficult to beat as it was the first time. Also, the OCD itself is not likely to be as strong or as upsetting. That is because you will be experienced in fighting OCD, and because the skills you have learned will continue to help you. Usually any attempts by OCD to sneak back in can be dealt with quickly and easily if you have a plan of action ready to go! That's what we'll help you to do in this chapter. The worksheets will become your action plan for what to do if OCD tries to reappear.

WHEN MIGHT OCD TRY TO REAPPEAR?

One of the main times when OCD might try to reappear in your life is when you are feeling stressed or worried. So the first items to put into your action plan are some ideas of when OCD might try to reappear.

Think for a moment about what sorts of stressful, worrying or difficult things might be coming up in your life.

- Do you have school exams coming up?

- Are you going to be moving house or changing school?

- Are you planning to leave school and find a job or go to university?

- Do you already have a job that is difficult or stressful?

- Do you frequently have ups and downs with friends or family members that you find difficult or stressful?

- Do you think there might be some other changes taking place in your life soon, such as a new brother or sister being born, a new pet, or an old pet who is very sick?

Try to think about positive changes as well as negative ones. Even though positive changes are usually good for us, *any* change can be a little bit stressful, and this is a common time when OCD might try to reappear.

Once you have come up with some ideas about possible things that might happen in your life, put them down in Box A on Worksheet 15.1.

An action plan for the future – Part I

What to do if OCD tries to reappear in my life

Box A

Sometimes OCD will try to reappear when you are experiencing changes, or are having a difficult or stressful time. Some possible things coming up in my life are:

These are times when it might be particularly important to be aware of OCD.

Box B

What might OCD look like? Will the same obsessions and compulsions return? Will new obsessions or compulsions return? The symptoms that might return are:

To help me recognize OCD, I need to remember that obsessions are:

and compulsions are:

Some of the things that I might do or say if OCD does reappear are:

How could others help me to recognize OCD? What could they do or say that I would find helpful?

✓

Box C

Face up to the worry as soon as you can. Use Worksheet 15.2 to help you design an E/RP task to face up to the worry. Remember this is the worksheet that you have used before in overcoming your OCD.

Who might be able to help you with doing some more E/RP tasks?

How could they help you?

What other methods might be helpful (e.g. bossing back OCD using helpful thoughts)?

WHAT MIGHT OCD LOOK LIKE IF IT TRIES TO REAPPEAR?

One of the most important ways to stay on top of OCD is to be aware of what it might look like if it does try to reappear in your life. What will the symptoms of OCD be like then?

- Do you think that the same thoughts and worries that you've had before might come back again?

- Or do you think that a new thought or worry might come into your mind?

There is some research that shows us that OCD in young people can take on different forms. For example, someone who used to be worried about dirt or germs and had to wash his hands to try to get rid of this worry might instead start to worry about something bad happening to someone in his family. To get rid of this new worry, he might have to count the number of red cars that go past his house from 8 a.m. until 9 a.m. in the morning.

To help you think about what new OCD might look like, think about what has happened to you in the past. Has your OCD tended to remain the same, or has it changed over time? It is sometimes easier to recognize OCD when it stays the same. But if your OCD does change, then use what you know about OCD to recognize it. Remind yourself of what obsessions and compulsions are (see page 22). By remembering how to define obsessions and compulsions, you can stay alert to OCD reappearing.

Think about these other ways in which you will know that OCD is trying to reappear:

- Will you have less time to spend with your friends than you did before?

- Will you want to spend more time by yourself?

- Will you find that you are more irritable with others than you used to be?

- Do you need other people to do things just the way you want them done?

Turn again to Worksheet 15.1 and in Box B write down what OCD might look like if it does try to reappear, and how you might recognize it.

Sometimes it is easier for other people to recognize OCD sooner than it is for you to recognize it yourself. This might sound a little bit silly, but because OCD rituals can be done very quickly sometimes, it might not feel like OCD. However, someone who knows you well might see that you have suddenly started doing some small rituals or compulsions again. How can they help you to recognize that OCD is trying to reappear? What might it be helpful for them to say or do? It is important to think about this and, if possible, to talk about this *now*, while you are developing your action plan.

WHAT OTHER THINGS CAN I DO?

Once you have recognized that OCD is trying to sneak back into your life, the next thing to do is to act early! The sooner you do something to get rid of OCD again, the easier it will be, and the less likely it will be that OCD will take a hold.

REMEMBER

Don't try to avoid the OCD. Don't try to pretend that it is not there, or that it will go away on its own. That is very unlikely to happen. In fact, if you wait around and hope that the OCD will go away on its own, it is more likely to get stronger while you are waiting.

What should you do? That depends a little bit on what sort of symptoms you have, and on what you found most helpful last time. One of the most useful things to do to prevent OCD from returning is to remember exactly what it was that helped you get better the first time.

- What were the most useful things you learned?

- What were the most helpful strategies you learned?

If the OCD thoughts that reappear aren't very strong, and you do not feel the need to do any compulsions, then maybe it will be enough to just recognize that OCD thoughts are popping up. But you can ignore them and carry on doing whatever you should be doing.

It is more likely that you will need to re-use some of the other skills that you have learned, particularly exposure and response prevention exercises (remember it's called E/RP for short). The steps to take then are just the same as those you have used before (see Chapter 9). Face up to the worry as soon as you can! Remember the steps to take in facing up to OCD worries:

A step-by-step guide to completing your E/RP exercise

- Step 1. Use Worksheet 15.2 to write down your chosen difficulty from your OCD ladder, and your E/RP exercise designed to expose you to your fears.

- Step 2. Rate how anxious you feel about not doing what OCD wants you to do, using your 'anxiety thermometer'.

- Step 3. Decide what your parent or carer can do to help you.

- Step 4. Start your E/RP exercise.

- Step 5. Rate your feeling of anxiety with the 'anxiety thermometer' every few minutes. Your aim is to record it until it comes right down.

- Step 6. Keep repeating this task for as many trials as it takes to stop causing you anxiety.

- Step 7. Re-rate your anxiety level on your OCD ladder.

Worksheet 15.2 can help you with deciding how to do your E/RP. It might be helpful to photocopy more of these worksheets for times in the future when you may need them.

An action plan for the future – Part II

> ### What to do if OCD tries to reappear in my life

What is OCD telling you to do?					
What is your E/RP exercise going to be?					
Rate how you feel about not doing what OCD wants (0–10).					
What can your parent or carer do to help?					
Record below what happens to your feelings of anxiety					

Trial	Your exercise is?	1 min	5 mins	15 mins	30 mins	60 mins

Now rate again how you feel about not doing what OCD wants (0–10).

It is also important to think about what other help you might need in doing some E/RP tasks again. Is there a particular person who would be good to help? Is it the same person who helped you last time? Would you like someone new to help you? Very often, the more support you have, the easier it is to overcome OCD quickly. What could this person do or say that would be helpful in doing an E/RP task? The more that other people say 'no' to OCD, the easier it is for you to do the same.

Finally, are there other strategies you learned that might make doing E/RP again easier?

- Was it helpful to think helpful thoughts to 'fight back' against the OCD?

- Was it helpful to 'put your thoughts on trial' or 'make a responsibility pie-chart'?

If you have found some things helpful in the past, the chances are that they will be helpful again. The more you remember to use the skills that you have learned, the easier it will be to stay on top of the OCD. Finish off your action plan by noting down some of the strategies that you found most helpful (Use Box C on Worksheet 15.1).

WHAT GOALS DO I HAVE FOR MY LIFE?

OCD has probably taken up a fair bit of your time until now. An important part of keeping OCD at bay is to use the extra time that you have got to do something else with your life. What other goals do you have?

- Do you want to spend more time with friends?

- Would you like to look for a part-time job to give you some extra money while you are studying?

- Do you want to repeat some exams that OCD made difficult for you the first time around?

- Do you want to go and see more movies?

- Do you want to learn how to make movies?

- Do you want to take a dance class or join a sports team?

You deserve to reward yourself for the hard work that you've put in by doing something for yourself now, and making it something that you will enjoy or something that you really want to do. By keeping yourself busy and involved with other things, there will be less opportunity for OCD to reappear.

SUMMARY

- It is normal that OCD might try to reappear in your life, or to become strong again.

- Don't worry about this, and don't be upset about it.

- Being prepared will help you to stay on top of OCD.

- Recognize OCD might be reappearing as soon as you can.

- Act early to get back on top.

- Use the same skills and strategies that you have already used to help you.

- Face up to the fears and worries, and fight the habits or compulsions!

- Use Worksheets 15.1 and 15.2 to help you.

- Fill the gap left by OCD. Take time to plan for some new hobbies or activities.

Now turn to the next part on page 185

ADVICE FOR PARENTS OR CARERS

This chapter has been about helping your child to make a plan for the future in case OCD tries to reappear. It is important for everyone to know that OCD might try to reappear, as this is not unusual. It does not mean that you have done anything wrong or that your child has done anything wrong. It simply reflects the natural course of OCD. By being prepared, no one need be worried or upset about some OCD symptoms coming back. If OCD does come back, it is not usually as strong as it was previously, and it is not usually as difficult to get back on top of it. That's because you and your child have now learned some important skills that help to overcome OCD.

There are several ways that you could help your child to stay on top of OCD. As with all other things in this book, though, the important thing to do first is to have an open discussion with your child about how you could best help. An ideal time to do this is right now, before the need arises. If you both have a plan in place, it is easier to follow a plan than to come up with something at the last minute. It might also save some arguments if you know what your child will find the most helpful. Some possibilities are as follows:

- Help your child to recognize OCD early. If you do notice some symptoms of OCD reappearing, how might it be helpful to communicate this to your child?

- Recognize that stressful or difficult times are ideal opportunities for OCD to try to reappear. This is because OCD is closely linked to anxiety, and stressful situations make us all feel anxious, even if they are positive stressors. Help your child to think about situations coming up that they might find stressful or difficult.

- Encourage your child to act early. The sooner you implement a plan to get back on top of OCD, the easier it is.

- Encourage your child to use the skills they have used in the past, particularly exposure and response prevention (E/RP). By facing up to the fear or worry early, it is less likely to be bothersome.

- Encourage your child to use any other strategies that they found particularly helpful. If they helped before, chances are they will be helpful again.

- Always remember that OCD is a distressing illness for your child to have. They are likely to benefit most from understanding and support to help them if a setback occurs.

OCD AND THE BIGGER PICTURE

In this part of the book we are going to consider some of the broader issues and questions that we often get asked by young people with OCD and their parents. We're going to focus on questions about family, about friends and about school. These are the sorts of issues that tend to be raised most often by young people with OCD. This part of the book will finish with a list of resources (books and websites) that you or your parents or helpers might like to look at for further information about OCD.

Chapter 16   # OCD and My Family

Only you and your family will really know how much OCD has changed people in the family, or changed the relationships that you have with people in the family. One thing is for sure, though – OCD can and does affect everyone.

HOW DOES OCD AFFECT FAMILIES?

The way OCD affects other people can be quite different. Some people in your family might feel angry or frustrated with OCD. Some people might feel sad about how difficult OCD makes things for you, others might not seem to care at all about how difficult things are for you. Some people might think you're just weird and ignore you and/or the OCD, while other people in your family might not even know you have OCD. Sometimes it might feel as though people in your family are upset or frustrated with you, rather than with the OCD. Maybe none of these things are true for you and your family, or maybe all of them are true to some extent at different times.

Every family is different, and no family will cope with OCD in the same way. Just as it is best for other family members to be patient and supportive of you in your fight against OCD, it is equally important that you are at times patient and supportive with them as they struggle to understand what you are experiencing.

YOU CAN OVERCOME OCD

It is important for you to always remember that OCD is an illness that you *can* recover from. The obsessions you experience and the compulsions you might do are not your own thoughts and behaviours. They are part of the illness, and you as a person are separate from the OCD. Although the impact of OCD on you and your family might sometimes feel huge, it doesn't need to remain that way. As you work to recover from OCD, it is likely that your family will begin to return to normal as well.

FREQUENTLY ASKED QUESTIONS (FAQS)

Should I tell my brother or sister that I have OCD?

There is no right or wrong answer to this question. The more support you have in fighting against OCD, the easier it will be for you. Even if your brother or sister doesn't know you have OCD, they are likely to know that *something* is wrong and you are not your usual self. OCD is an illness that affects everyone in the family, so it is usually helpful to explain OCD to your brother or sister, or ask one of your parents to explain it to them.

However, deciding whether or not to tell someone about your OCD depends on *your reasons* for wanting to tell them, and on how you think they are likely to take the news.

- If you feel that telling someone about your OCD is going to be helpful to you, or a relief for you not to have to keep it a secret any longer, then perhaps you should tell.

- If you feel that they might tease you, or tell other people that you have OCD, then perhaps it would be best to think about telling someone else instead.

Fighting OCD is a big job, and you want people around you who can help and support you in achieving your goals.

My father or mother is always yelling at me for doing a ritual, but I can't help it. What should I do?

OCD can raise all sorts of emotions in other family members, particularly parents. Many parents have told us that at times they feel they want to 'rescue' their child from OCD, while at other times they just feel like screaming from frustration and anger at OCD. If your parents seem to be yelling a lot when you do a ritual, it is probably because they are feeling really frustrated and perhaps unsure of how to best help you.

We suggest talking to your parents about how you feel. Try to find a time to talk when everyone is feeling calm and OCD is not bothering you. You might like them to help you fight OCD. You might want to ask your parent to read this book, or just the parent advice sections, or to read something else which might help to explain OCD to them. We have provided a list of books and websites in the final chapter of this book and some of these have been written for parents.

It would be so much easier for me if my mother or father would just tell me that everything is going to be OK. Can I ask for that?

Asking for reassurance is one of the most common compulsions that young people with OCD have. Look back at Chapter 10, 'Making Progress with Exposure and Response Prevention Exercises', if you want to find out more about this. Remember that any compulsion, however quickly you might be able to do it, keeps the OCD going. It is going to help you more if you are able to plan to stop this reassurance-seeking ritual using the E/RP skills that you have learned about already. As with fighting all other compulsions, this will become easier to do the more you practise.

Cutting down on asking for reassurance is likely to be something that you will need your parents to help you with, because they will also need to understand that giving you reassurance is not helpful in the longer term. They might like to re-read Chapter 10 to understand how best to help you.

I used to get on really well with my sister or brother, but now we hardly ever speak to each other. What can I do?

OCD can have a very negative effect on your life, and one of the things that can be badly affected is your relationship with other people. We also know that having close relationships with other people (family or friends) is important for helping you to feel good about yourself. Improving your relationships and spending more time with the people that you care about, as well as doing things that you enjoy, will be increasingly possible as you overcome your OCD.

Think about how you would like your relationship with your brother or sister to improve. Would you like to do more activities together? Would you like to spend more time talking to each other? Close relationships are usually developed and kept by time spent together, doing things that you both find interesting and enjoyable. Think about how you might do this with your brother or sister, and then perhaps talk to him or her about how you feel. They may have missed you as much as you've missed them and will welcome you bringing it up.

I'm worried that my younger sister or brother will get OCD if I have it. Is there anything I can do to make sure they don't get it?

Although OCD is an illness, it is not something that someone else can catch off you. No one really knows for sure why some young people get OCD and others don't. Although OCD is a little bit more likely to occur if someone else in your family has had it, this does not mean that other people in your family will definitely get it.

OCD is nobody's fault. There is nothing you can do that would make it more likely that anyone else will get OCD. Also, there is nothing you can do to stop them getting OCD if that is what is going to happen. All you can do is offer your support, and perhaps help them to overcome OCD if that's something they would like you to do.

Now turn to the next chapter on page 196

ADVICE FOR PARENTS OR CARERS

OCD is a condition that affects everyone in the family, not just the child who has it. Many parents have told us of the wide range of emotions they have experienced as they struggle with coming to terms with their child's OCD. For many parents, there is confusion and concern when initial symptoms of OCD appear. For some parents, coming to the realization that their child has OCD can be a relief, as a clear understanding of a diagnosis can help to gain a new perspective on changes in a child's mood and behaviour, and can open up avenues for help or support that weren't previously available. For others, it can lead to great sadness and even guilt for how they may have contributed to this illness in their child.

OCD is nobody's fault. It is not your fault that your child has OCD, and there is nothing that you could have done, or shouldn't have done, that would have made things different. Having OCD is just bad luck. Certainly there are some risk factors that may make someone more vulnerable to OCD than someone else. However, risk factors are just that – possible background factors that may slightly increase someone's risk of developing OCD, but in and of themselves they are rarely causative.

It is important that you are aware of your own feelings about your child's OCD, and are aware of what you may be communicating to your child. It is perfectly normal that you may at times feel angry, frustrated and upset by OCD. In fact, we have yet to meet a parent who hasn't experienced these emotions as a result of the OCD. However, it is rarely helpful that these feelings are communicated to your child. You need to find someone with whom you can share your feelings, such as a partner, a close friend, a sibling or parent of your own, or perhaps another parent that you know well. A problem shared can be a problem halved (at least for the time that you are sharing it with another).

Below we give some brief guidance for parents or carers, and these represent the issues that we think are most important and that are raised most often by parents. However, this is unlikely to cover all of the concerns, questions and/or feelings that you may have, and in the final chapter of this book we provide some books and websites that you may like to look at for additional information.

RECOGNIZE THAT YOUR CHILD AND OCD ARE TWO SEPARATE ENTITIES

Sometimes it is helpful to draw parallels between OCD and another illness like asthma or diabetes, or another problem like a broken leg. If your child had asthma for example, you would not be angry with them for coughing, and you would recognize that some changes may need to be made to family routines in order to help them cope with this illness in the best possible way. Similarly, if your child had a broken leg, it would at times be frustrating, but you would not be angry at them if they needed help in bathing, or getting up to their bedroom, or even getting ready for school.

By recognizing that OCD is an illness , it is easier to remain patient and supportive of your child, and to keep negative feelings about the OCD in check. As hard as it is for you as a parent or carer, it is many times harder for your child to have OCD.

LOOK AFTER YOURSELF

It is incredibly important that you take the time to look after yourself as well as the child. Many parents feel that they shouldn't take time for themselves when their child has OCD. However, in reality, the opposite is true. When a child has an illness like OCD, it is particularly important that you have your full energy resources, because you're likely to need to draw on them as you help the child. Looking after yourself is one of the most important ways in which you can help to look after the child. You are more likely to be able to remain patient and supportive if you are well rested and prioritize taking time out for yourself.

CHOOSE YOUR PRIORITIES CAREFULLY

When you are caring for a child with any sort of illness, it can be a time-consuming, difficult and exhausting job. If your child is very unwell, it is likely that you won't be able to successfully complete all of the tasks that you otherwise might if your child was not ill. Be prepared to prioritize your responsibilities, and recognize there are some things that will always need to be done, but there are others that can wait or be put on hold altogether. Allow some of the less important things to be put on hold while you focus on caring for and helping your child. Once the child recovers from OCD, you will have time again to pick up some of the things that you may have had to put aside.

ASK FOR HELP WHEN YOU NEED IT

There will be times in your experience of parenting a child with OCD where you just won't be able to do it all alone. When you feel that things might be too much, ask someone for help.

TELLING MEMBERS OF THE EXTENDED FAMILY ABOUT OCD

Some parents find a great deal of support in their extended family, others feel that it might have been better if extended family had never been told about a child's OCD. Deciding whether or not to tell other family members about your child's OCD is a decision that is best made together with the child. Extra support is always helpful, but extra stress is not. If you do decide to tell others, try to give them as much accurate information about OCD as possible so that they can understand what you and the child are experiencing.

IF YOU HAVE OCD OR ANOTHER ANXIETY DISORDER, CONSIDER WHAT HELP YOU MIGHT NEED

One of the most helpful things you can do for a child who has an illness like OCD is to seek help yourself if you also have OCD or an anxiety disorder. As we have discussed earlier in this book, the recommended treatments for OCD in adults are cognitive behaviour therapy (CBT) and SSRI medication. In seeking treatment yourself, you are providing your child with a role model, and showing them that overcoming an illness like OCD is an important priority in your family. If you participate in CBT yourself, you will also be learning more about anxiety and OCD, and about ways of managing this. This information may be helpful when you are helping your child recover.

MAINTAIN LIMITS ON ACCEPTABLE AND UNACCEPTABLE BEHAVIOUR

It can be very confusing sometimes to know when your child's behaviour is driven by OCD, or when he or she may be simply misbehaving and pushing the limits. The fact that your child has OCD, does not give them a licence to be rude or aggressive, or to ignore family rules and responsibilities. There can never be any absolutes, because OCD will inevitably impact upon your child's home life, and some allowances will need to be made to the roles and responsibilities that they take on within the family.

For example, it is not uncommon for a young person with fears about germs and contamination to refuse to touch or prepare food or to touch crockery or cutlery. It may be sensible to relieve them of chores that involve meal preparation while you together agree on what goals you are focusing on to overcome the OCD.

It is also normal that when your child is feeling fed-up or angry or frustrated with the OCD that they should want to lash out. However, as with any behaviour that is unacceptable, we would recommend discussing the behaviour, reminding your child of the boundaries and limits that operate within your family, and establishing consequences for violating these boundaries.

A word of caution is appropriate here. If you are going to establish consequences, be prepared to follow through on them. Managing child behaviour in the context of caring for a child with OCD is never an easy task, and there may not be any right or wrong answers. If you end up being wrong, then try to learn from mistakes and talk about them with your child.

REMEMBER YOU DON'T HAVE TO BE PERFECT

There is no such thing as a perfect parent, and certainly no one comes prepared for every parenting challenge that their children might present them with. Having a child with OCD will raise all sorts of new challenges that you may never have encountered before. Be gentle on yourself and have realistic expectations for success and failure in managing new and complex problems that may arise.

FOCUS ON THINGS OTHER THAN OCD

When you are parenting a child with OCD, it is all too easy to begin to focus just on OCD each day. Try to maintain a focus on other things, and in particular on other behaviour in your child that is not OCD. Remember to praise and reward the behaviours that you would like to see more of.

GIVE ATTENTION TO OTHER FAMILY MEMBERS

Everyone in the family will want your time and attention at some point. Although a child who is ill is likely to take up more time and attention than may be their fair share, this is normal, and it is necessary that you give them extra time at all stages of the illness. However, it is important that you explain this to your other children and perhaps to your partner. Explain to them why it is important. Where possible, and with your child's permission, talk to your other children about OCD and encourage them to understand the special needs that their sibling may have at this time. Reassure them that they are still loved, and look for opportunities to spend some quality time with them without the distraction of your OCD child. Maintain as much of the family routine as you can. As your child with OCD begins to recover, you will find that you have more time to shift back to other family members.

Chapter 17 OCD, School and Friends

OCD AND SCHOOL

OCD and school can be a really difficult issue. OCD may not affect your schoolwork or your school life very much or at all, or it may affect it so much that going to school and/or going to certain classes can be really difficult.

Even if attendance is not difficult, OCD can sometimes make it very hard for young people to concentrate properly on what is being learned, particularly if obsessions are bothersome at school.

Rituals can also make it hard to complete certain pieces of work. For example, repeating rituals can make it very difficult to read or write some-

thing if you feel the urge to re-read or re-write, or if you have to do something perfectly. The need for reassurance can mean that you are repeatedly asking teachers questions or asking for help.

Consider as early as possible whether or not you want people at school to know about your OCD. If OCD is affecting your schoolwork or school life in any way, it can be helpful to talk to someone. The goals of telling school about your OCD should be to help you limit the negative effect that OCD has on you while at school, and to provide help and support for the school situations that OCD makes particularly difficult.

There may be a particular teacher or person whom you trust more than others, or there may be a particular person at the school (e.g. a school nurse or counsellor) whose job it is to help young people who are experiencing all sorts of different problems.

Some of the ways in which schools might be able to help a young person with OCD include:

- temporarily arranging alternative rooms to use if particular rooms are triggers for OCD obsessions or rituals (e.g. the sports room, or the science rooms)

- providing a safe place for you to go to calm down if you are feeling particularly upset or stressed

- arranging for special consideration to be given for important exams

- allowing extra time to be given in exams

- making special arrangements for the completion of homework

- support in doing E/RP tasks at school

- providing a particular person with whom you can speak

- arranging a system of communication so that you can let teachers know in subtle ways when you need some extra help or support

- showing increased patience and understanding of rituals that are done at school.

Unfortunately, there is variation in how schools and school personnel will respond to knowing about OCD. We hope that your school will be very supportive and understanding. However, you need to be prepared for the fact that they might not seem to understand, and you and your family might need to 'make an issue of it'. In our experience this is rare, but possible. If you have spoken to your doctor or a therapist about your OCD, then they may be able to help you in speaking to the school, and in making arrangements that are right for your needs. Whenever special arrangements are made, it is best to view these as temporary, and it should be one of your goals to try to minimize the impact that OCD has on your schoolwork and school life.

Recognize that it can take some time to achieve the goals that you have set for yourself, and that young people who experience OCD may need longer to complete their education than others. The most important thing should be your recovery from OCD. It is always possible to take your exams another time. Education is not a race, but a life-long process.

OCD AND YOUR FRIENDS

Having relationships with friends and other people your own age is an important part of life. Friends can be one of the greatest supports you have when stressful things happen in life. OCD can affect all areas of life, including your friendships. If your OCD is mild and is really only bothersome for you at home, then perhaps your friends will not even know that you have OCD. However, if your OCD affects you at school as well as at home, then it is likely that your friends will recognize that something is bothering or upsetting you. Perhaps you've had severe OCD for quite some time, and haven't been able to take the time to maintain friendships with others.

The more you are able to spend enjoyable time with friends, or to re-build your friendships, the happier you will feel, and the less bothersome OCD will feel. In coming up with some goals for yourself in your recovery from OCD, involving yourself in hobbies or activities you enjoy and spending time with friends should be on your list.

TELLING YOUR FRIENDS ABOUT OCD

Many young people have told us that they often feel worried or anxious about telling their friends they have OCD. Most of the time, if they are true friends, they will remain loyal and supportive. The more accurate information you can give them, the easier it will be for them to understand what is happening for you. If your friends don't respond well to you telling them that you have OCD, then perhaps they are not the sort of people that you would like to have as your friends anyway.

However, it is important to consider carefully whether you *do* want to tell your friends about OCD. If you decide that you do, then consider when and how you want to tell them. It might feel quite risky to share a secret like OCD with someone. Think about what you know about your friends.

- Are they the sort of people that you can trust?

- Have you told them anything really personal before?

- Do they tease you if you tell them something personal?

- Do they keep secrets well?

If you are not sure of the answers to these questions, perhaps you could 'test the waters' by telling them something else personal about yourself to see how they react. It is your decision about who to tell and when; but remember, the more support you have in fighting your OCD, the easier it will seem.

OCD is not an uncommon illness. We discussed earlier in the book that OCD could affect up to 2 young people in every 100. It may be that one of your friends has OCD also, but has never told you about it. Or they may know someone else with OCD. It could be reassuring for you to know of someone else who has OCD.

Chapter 18	# Where to Go for More Information

BOOKS FOR YOUNG PEOPLE

Wells, J. (2006). *Touch and Go Joe: An Adolescent's Experience of OCD.* Jessica Kingsley Publishers, London.

An honest and amusing account of a 15-year-old's battle with OCD. This book will be of interest to anyone who has suffered from (or knows someone else who has suffered from) OCD, including children and adolescents, teachers, psychologists, psychiatrists, mental health professionals, parents and carers.

ISBN: 978-1843103912

March, J.S. and Benton, M. (2007) *Talking Back to OCD: The Program That Helps Kids and Teens Say 'No Way' – and Parents Say 'Way to Go'.* Guilford Press, New York, NY.

Dr March tackles the bewilderment and isolation felt by many families, highlighting the fact that OCD is nobody's fault and emphasizing that recovery is possible.

ISBN: 978-1593853556

Veale, D. and Willson, R. (2005) *Overcoming Obsessive Compulsive Disorder*. Robinson Publishing, London.

This accessible guide explains how readers can reduce the distress of intrusive thoughts, face fears, avoided situations and overcome compulsions. This book is written for adults, but older adolescents might

find this helpful. There are two chapters for parents that address OCD in children and young people.
ISBN: 978-18431199368

BOOKS FOR CHILDREN

Wagner, A.P. (2004). *Up and Down the Worry Hill: A Children's Book About Obsessive Compulsive Disorder and its Treatment*. Lighthouse Press, Deerfield Beach, FL.
An illustrated book designed to help parents and professionals explain OCD to younger children through the story of 'Casey', a young boy with OCD.
ISBN: 978-0967734767

Wever, C. and Phillips, N. (1994). *The Secret Problem*. Shrink-rap Press, West Concord, NSW.
An illustrated book that describes OCD in clear and simple language to help children, teenagers and their parents understand OCD and its treatment.
ISBN:978–0646220635

BOOKS FOR PARENTS OR CARERS

Chansky, T.E. (2001). *Freeing Your Child from Obsessive-Compulsive Disorder*. Three Rivers Press, New York, NY.
Proven techniques parents can use to help their children break the debilitating cycles of obsessive compulsive disorder and take control of their own lives. In this book, Dr Tamar Chansky offers step-by-step ways to guide children out of OCD and help parents cope every step of the way.
ISBN: 978-0812931174

Wagner, A.P. (2000). *What to Do when your Child has Obsessive-Compulsive Disorder: Strategies and Solutions*. Lighthouse Press, Deerfield Beach, FL.
In plain language, Dr Wagner speaks to the many and complex concerns parents of children with OCD have, always with the goal to

help minimize the impact of OCD on the child and family. A very practical guide for parents.
ISBN: 978-0967734712

Waltz, M. (2000). *Obsessive Compulsive Disorder: Help for Children and Adolescents*. O'Reilly Media, Sebastopol, CA.
Written by a woman with OCD who has two children with OCD, this book provides information about OCD, its diagnosis and treatment and advice for working with schools.
ISBN: 978-1565927582

WEBSITES

http://aftoc.club.fr/index.php
Association Française de personnes souffrant de Troubles Obsessionels et Compulsifs – The French Association for People Suffering from Obsessive-Compulsive Problems. A website for sufferers and ex-sufferers of OCD and their families in France . (Accessed 7 April 2008)

www.abct.org
Association for Behavioral and Cognitive Therapies, New York. (Accessed 10 March 2008)
The Association of Behavioural and Cognitive Therapies is a not-for-profit international membership organization for people who study, practice and/or conduct research in cognitive-behavioural therapy. It has a 'Find a Therapist' resource for the public in the US.

www.asociaciontoc.org/asociacion/introduccion.hm
Asociacion de Trastornos Obsesivo-Compulsivos. A Spanish organization dedicated to research and education about OCD. (Accessed 7 April 2008)

www.arcvic. com.au
Anxiety Recovery centre Victoria (ARCVic)
A Website for people who suffer from anxiety disorders, and for their families, relatives and friends. (Accessed 7 April 2008)

www.ocdaction.org.uk

OCD ACTION Help and Information Line: 0845 390 6232 (UK)
The website gives advice and information about OCD and related
conditions. There is an area of the site for children with OCD and their
families. This site also details the contact information for worldwide
OCD resources: http://www.ocdaction.org.uk/ocdaction/index.
asp?id=424 (Accessed 10 March 2008)

www.ocdhope.com

OCD Hope – Florida. Information about OCD, its treatment and
support groups. (Accessed 7 April 2008)

www.ocdireland.org

OCD Ireland is national organization for people with Obsessive
Compulsive Disorders (OCD) and the related disorders of Body
Dysmorphic Disorder (BDD) and Trichotillomania. (Accessed 7 April
2008)

www.ocdmanitoba.ca/welcome/htm

OCD Center Manitoba, Inc., is a non-profit organization that provides
support, education, and information to members, family, friends,
and professionlas, about Obessive Compulsive Disorder (OCD).
(Accessed 7 April 2008)

www.ocfchicago.org

Obsessive Compulsive Foundation of Chicago serves adults and
children with OCD, their families, and the mental health professionals
who treat them. It is the only Chicago-area organization dedicated to
OCD. (Accessed 7 April 2008)

www.ocdyouth.iop.kcl.ac.uk

This website offers information about OCD and its treatment in young
people. It provides other resources for young people suffering from
OCD and their parents. (accessed 10 March 2008)

www.ocfoundation.org

This website offers information about OCD, links to other resources,
and information about the support available for people suffering from

obsessive compulsive disorder (an American website). (accessed 10 March 2008)

www.tsa.org.uk

The Tourette Syndrome (TS) Association provides information about TS to individuals, professionals and agencies in the fields of health care, education and government. The website includes links to other sites, information about help lines, books, journal articles, and events relating to Tourette Syndrome. (accessed 10 March 2008)

www.youngminds.org.uk

Young Minds is a UK national charity for children and parents of children with mental health problems. They offer information and advice to parents, young people and professionals about mental health problems, how to cope with mental health problems, best practice, current campaigns, and information about child and adolescent mental health services. (accessed 10 March 2008)

www.youthinmind.co.uk

This website offers advice and information to young people, parents and teachers about mental health issues for young people. There is also a search engine that you can use to find specialist mental health services in the UK. (accessed 10 March 2008)

Appendix

QUESTIONNAIRE*

TO BE COMPLETED BY THE YOUNG PERSON

NAME: _____

Date:_____ Age: _____ Sex: Male/Female

Part 1

Each of the following questions asks you about things or 'habits' you feel you have to do although you may know that they do not make sense. Sometimes, you may try to stop from doing them but this might not be possible. You might feel worried or angry or frustrated until you have finished what you have to do. An example of a habit like this may be the need to wash your hands over and over again even though they are not really dirty, or the need to count up to a special number (e.g. 6 or 10) while you do certain things.

Please answer each question by putting a circle around the number that best describes how much you agree with the statement, or how much you think it is true of you. Please answer each item, without spending too much time on any one item. There are no right or wrong answers.

Example	Not at all	Somewhat	A lot
I feel that I must check and check again that the stove is turned off, even if I don't want to do so.	1	(2)	3

*   This questionnaire is the Children's Obsessive Compulsive Inventory (CHOCI). It was designed by Professor Roz Shafran and colleagues. See: Uher, R., Heyman, I., Turner, C. and Shafran, R. (2007) 'Self-, parent-report and interview measures of obsessive-compulsive disorder in children and adolescents.' *Journal of Anxiety Disorders*, published online 13 October 2007.

How much do you agree with each of the following statements?	Not at all	Somewhat	A lot
1. I spend far too much time washing my hands over and over again.	1	2	3
2. I feel I must do ordinary/everyday things exactly the same way, every time I do them.	1	2	3
3. I spend a lot of time every day checking things over and over and over again.	1	2	3
4. I often have trouble finishing things because I need to make absolutely sure that everything is exactly right.	1	2	3
5. I spend far too much time arranging my things in order.	1	2	3
6. I need someone to tell me things are alright over and over again.	1	2	3
7. If I touch something with one hand, I feel I absolutely *must* touch the same thing with the other hand, in order to make things even and equal.	1	2	3
8. I always count, even when doing ordinary things.	1	2	3
9. If I have a 'bad thought', I always have to make sure that I immediately have a 'good thought' to cancel it out.	1	2	3
10. I am often very late because I keep on repeating the same action, over and over again.	1	2	3

Please turn the page and continue

Rate your compulsions

Please try to think about the three *most* upsetting habits that you feel you have to do and can't stop. For example, feeling that you have to wash your hands far too often, or repeating the same action over & over, or constantly checking that the doors and windows are shut properly.

1. ....

2. ....

3. ....

(a) How much time do you spend doing these habits? Please circle the answer that best describes you.

0	1	2	3	4
None	Less than 1 hr. a day (occasionally)	1–3 hrs. a day (part of a morning or afternoon)	3–8 hrs. a day (about half the time you're awake)	More than 8 hrs. a day (almost all the time you're awake)

(b) How much do these habits get in the way of school or doing things with friends? Please circle the answer that best describes you.

0	1	2	3	4
Not at all	A little	Somewhat	A lot	Almost always

(c) How would you feel if prevented from carrying out your habits? How upset would you become? Please circle the answer that best describes you.

0	1	2	3	4
Not at all	A little	Somewhat	A lot	Totally

(d) How much do you try to fight the upsetting habits? Please circle the answer that best describes you.

0	1	2	3	4
I always try to resist	I try to resist most of the time	I make some effort to resist	Even though I want to, I don't try to resist	I don't resist at all

(e) How strong is the feeling that you have to carry out the habits? Please circle the answer that best describes you.

0	1	2	3	4
Not strong	Mild pressure to carry out habits	Strong pressure to carry out habits; hard to control	Very strong pressure to carry out habits; very hard to control	Extreme pressure to carry out habits; impossible to control

(f) How much have you been avoiding doing anything, going any place, or being with anyone because of your upsetting habits? Please circle the answer that best describes you.

0	1	2	3	4
Not at all	A little	Somewhat	A lot	Almost always

NAME: _____

Part 2

In this section, each of the questions asks you about *thoughts, ideas, or pictures* that keep coming into your mind even though you do not want them to do so. They may be unpleasant, silly, or embarrassing. For example, some young people have the repeated thought that germs or dirt are harming them or other people, or that something unpleasant may happen to them or someone special to them. These are thoughts that keep coming back, over and over again, even though you do not want them.

Please answer each question by putting a circle around the number that best describes how much you agree with the statement, or how much you think it is true of you. Please answer each item, without spending too much time on any one item. There are no right or wrong answers.

Example	Not at all	Somewhat	A lot
I often have the same upsetting thought about death over and over again.	1	2	(3)

How much do you agree with each of the following statements?	Not at all	Somewhat	A lot
1. I can't stop thinking upsetting thoughts about an accident.	1	2	3
2. I often have bad thoughts that make me feel like a terrible person.	1	2	3
3. Upsetting thoughts about my family being hurt go round and round in my head and stop me from concentrating.	1	2	3
4. I always have big doubts about whether I've made the right decision, even about stupid little things.	1	2	3
5. I can't stop upsetting thoughts about death from going round in my head, over and over again.	1	2	3
6. I often have mean thoughts about other people that I feel are terrible, over and over again.	1	2	3
7. I often have horrible thoughts about going crazy.	1	2	3
8. I keep on having frightening thoughts that something terrible is going to happen and it will be my fault.	1	2	3
9. I'm very frightened that I will think something (or do something) that will upset God.	1	2	3
10. I'm always worried that my mean thoughts about other people are as wicked as actually doing mean things to them.	1	2	3

Please turn the page and continue

Rate your obsessions

Please list the three most severe *thoughts* that you often have *and can't stop thinking about*. For example, thinking about hurting someone, or thinking bad things about God.

1. ....

2. ....

3. ....

(g) How much time do you spend thinking about these things? Please circle the answer that best describes you.

0	1	2	3	4
None	Less than 1 hr. a day (occasionally)	1–3 hrs. a day (part of a morning or afternoon)	3–8 hrs. a day (about half the time you're awake)	More than 8 hrs. a day (almost all the time you're awake)

(h) How much do these thoughts get in the way of school or doing things with friends? Please circle the answer that best describes you.

0	1	2	3	4
Not at all	A little	Somewhat	A lot	Extreme

(i) How much do these thoughts bother or upset you? Please circle the answer that best describes you.

0	1	2	3	4
Not at all	A little	Somewhat	A lot	Extreme

(j) How hard do you try to stop the thoughts or ignore them? Please circle the answer that best describes you.

0	1	2	3	4
I always try to resist	I try to resist most of the time	I make some effort to resist	Even though I want to, I don't try to resist	I don't resist at all

(k) When you try to fight the thoughts, can you beat them? How much control do you have over the thoughts? Please circle the answer that best describes you.

0	1	2	3	4
Complete control	Much control	Moderate control	Little control	No control

(l) How much have you been avoiding doing anything, going any place, or being with anyone because of your thoughts? Please circle the answer that best describes you.

0	1	2	3	4
Not at all	A little	Somewhat	A lot	Almost always

You can now score your questionnaire.

In order to find out how much compulsions are interfering in your life, score the compulsion section by simply add up the numbers that you have circled for each of these questions.

(a) how much time you spend doing compulsions,

(b) how much the compulsions get in the way of you doing things,

(c) how upset you would feel if you were prevented from doing the compulsions,

(d) how much do you try to fight the compulsions,

(e) how strong is the feeling that you have to carry out the compulsions, and

(f) how much have you been avoiding things, places or people because of the compulsions.

In order to find out how much obsessions are interfering in your life, score the obsession section by simply add up the numbers that you have circled for each of these questions.

(g) how much time you spend thinking about the obsessions,

(h) how much the thoughts get in the way of you doing things,

(i) how much the thoughts bother you or upset you,

(j) how hard you try to stop the thoughts or ignore them,

(k) how much control do you have over the thoughts, and

(l) how much have you been avoiding things, places or people because of the thoughts.

Put your score in the space below.

Compulsions interference score: _____

Obsessions interference score: _____

TOTAl interference score: _____
(add up the compulsions and obsessions score)

If your total score is 12 or more, it may be helpful for you to speak to your doctor about OCD. Take a copy of this questionnaire if you think that you have OCD but you are not sure. He or she may suggest that you see a clinical psychologist or a psychiatrist who may be able to help you further.

INDEX

Note: page numbers in *italics* refer to diagrams, tables and worksheets.

action plans *see* OCD action plans
acupuncture 35
adult OCD 28, 194
advocate role 67
aggressive behaviour 118, 194–5
anger 114, 194–5
anxiety 28–9, 59, 69–79
  definition 69
  exposure and response prevention for 95, 100, 103, *104*, 106, 108, 110–14, *112*, 116, 121, 124, 179
  failure to reduce 121, 124
  and family collusion with OCD 117–18
  getting used to (habituation to) 73, *76*, 77, 79, 95

harmful effects of 72
helpful 72, 78
identifying your 50
measurement 69, 73–5, *74*, 78–9, 84, 92, 100, 103, 108, 179
measurement over time 75–7, *76*
physical effects of 70, 71, *71*, 79
rating your compulsions for 84, 86, *86*, *88*, 89, 92
short-term relief of 48, *48*, *51-2*, 53, 117–18
unhelpful 72
see also worry
anxiety disorders, parental 194
anxiety graphs (for drawing out your anxiety) 75–7, *76*, 111-12, *112*
anxiety thermometers (for measuring your anxiety) 69, 73–5, *74*

77–8, 84, 92, 100, 103, 108, 179
autism spectrum disorders 37
'avoidance' behaviours 21, 53, 65, 67, 95, 108, 116, 124, 167

'bad person' complex 24
behavioural experiments 60, 127, 157–8, 159–72, *162*, *165*
  carrying out 161–4, *162*
  making sense of *169*
  overcoming problems with 164–7
  progress checks 170
  resistance to 165
  step-by-step guide to 163
bullying 87, *88*

carers *see* parents and carers
case stories 20–3

case stories *cont.*
  behavioural experiments
    160, 164, *165*, 166–7,
    167, 171–2
  breaking OCD's rules 98,
    99, *99*
  exposure and prevention
    response 102, *102*,
    126–7, 130
  first appointments with
    your doctor 34
  measuring anxiety 74–5
  OCD diaries 83, *83*
  OCD ladders 87, *88*, *99*
  OCD timetables 62
  the OCD trap 49–50, *51*
  'putting OCD on trial'
    technique 148–9, *149*
  responsibility pie-chart
    152–3, *153–4*
  telling people about your
    OCD 32
causes of OCD 30, 191,
  192
CBT *see* cognitive
  behaviour therapy
certainty, need for 134,
  141–2, 146
change
  fear of 61, 164–5
  pushing for 130
  and relapse 174, 183
checking rituals 20–2, 83,
  83, 126
child mental health workers
  37
child psychiatrists 33
Children's Obsessive
  Compulsive Inventory
  (CHOCI) 62–4, 170,
  206–15

chunking tasks 92
citalopram 38
clarifier role 66
cleanliness rituals *see*
  contamination
  phobias/cleanliness
  rituals
clinical psychologists 33
clomipramine 38
cognitive behaviour
  therapists 18, 33
cognitive behaviour therapy
  (CBT) 15–18, 33–4,
  37–9, 59, 61, 194
  defining 40–5
  duration of therapy 43
  top-up sessions 39
collaborative approaches
  65–6
compulsions 21–2, 28–9,
  31, 65
  about offending people
    49–50, *51*
  and anxiety 74, 75–6, *76*
  checking behaviours
    20–2, 83, *83*, 126
  common 22, *23*
  of counting 23, 108
  definition 21, 27, 46
  delaying 98
  getting caught up in your
    child's 57, 116–18
  hidden/covert 124
  identifying your child's
    55, *56*
  measuring 62–4, 170
  mental rituals 21–2, 28,
    55, 108
  new 125, 165, 177–8
  and OCD action plans *90*

and the OCD trap
    48–50, *48*, *51–2*, 53,
    55
  overcoming with
    behavioural
    experiments *162*,
    163, 165, 171
  overcoming with helpful
    thoughts 140–1
  overcoming with
    exposure and
    response prevention
    94–6, 98–100, *101–2*,
    102, 104, *104*, 108,
    120–1, 124–7, *128*
  performing in a different
    place 99
  performing variations of
    98
  rating your 206–9,
    214–15
  recording on OCD
    ladders 84–6, *86*, 92
  recovery from 188
  'reducing' obsessions by
    performing 21, 27,
    28, 48, *48*, 50, *51–2*,
    53, 74, 132, 146
  relapsing into 177–8
  repeating rituals 196–7
  and school 196–7
  shortening 98
  shouting at children for
    189
  unconscious 124
  see also reassurance
    seeking
contamination
  phobias/cleanliness
  rituals 62, 65, 98, 99,

99, 117, 124, 160, 164, 166–7, *167*, 171–2, 194

control
  issues of 118, 134, 172
  taking back from OCD 139–40
coping ability, underestimation of your 72
counselling 35
counsellors 171–2
counting compulsions 23, 108
'crazy', feelings of being 29

danger, overestimation of 72, 78
death, fear of 49–50, *51*
defining OCD 13, 19–29
depression 35, 37
diagnosing OCD 13–16, 17, 25, 29–30
  advice for carers/parents 28
  guidelines 17, 18
  parental reactions to 192
  professional diagnosis 25, 30, 37
  and the short obsessive compulsive scale *26*
  telling people about (disclosure) 32, 36, 55, 188–9, 194, 197–8, 199–200
diaries, OCD 59, 80–4, *82–3*
discipline 194–5
disclosing your OCD 32, 36, 55, 188–9

to the extended family 194
to friends 199–200
to schools 197–8
to siblings 188–9
disgust 28
doctors 14–15, 197
  getting help from 32–3, 34, 36–7
  guide to going to see 32–3
  and NICE guidelines 18
dopamine 39

embarrassment 29, 31–2, 65
encouragement 108
exams
  accommodating your OCD and 197
  compulsions involving 102, *102*
expert patients 17, 46–58
exposure and response prevention (E/RP) 38, 59, 61, 94–109, 158
  and OCD ladders 84, 85, 89, 92, 95, 97, *97*, 99–100, *99*, 103, *104*, 108, 110–11, 113–14, 116–18, 130, 158, 179
  anxiety graphs 111–12, *112*
  avoiding the exercises 120–1
  and behavioural experiments 160, 161, 164–5

defining 94–5, 108
designing exercises 95–6
doing your first exercise 99–100, *101*, *102*
making progress with 110–19
moving on from your first exercise 105
and the OCD timetable *122–3*
overcoming difficulties 113, 120–31
progress monitoring 103, *104*, 106, 108, 114
for reassurance seeking 189
for relapse 179, *180* 181, 183
and resistant anxiety ratings 121, 124
at school 197
step-by-step guides to 100, 111, 179

families 187–95
  disclosing your OCD to 188–9, 194
  effects of OCD on 57–8, 187
  extended 194
  involvement in OCD (accommodating OCD) 113–14, 116–19, 130
  see also parents and carers
family therapy 35
fear 61, 130
  avoiding confrontation of your 65, 67

family therapy *cont.*
of OCD symptoms 28, 29
'fight or flight' response 69, 70, 78
fluoxetine 38
fluvoxamine 38
frequently asked questions (FAQs) 188–91
friends 198–200

generalized anxiety disorder 37
goals 181–2
guilt 28, 30, 192

habits, annoying 14–15
see also compulsions
help, asking for 193
herbal remedies 35
hypnosis 35

imagination 95–6
intrusive thoughts *see* unpleasant/intrusive thoughts

magical thinking 87, 133, 140–1, 146
maintaining progress 173–83
measuring OCD 62–4, 170, 206–15
medication 15–17, 34, 35, 38–9, 194
dosage 39
response time 39
side-effects 38–9

mental rituals 21–2, 28, 108
signs of 55
monitor role 67
motivator role 67

National Institute for Health and Clinical Excellence (NICE), guidelines 18, 36, 38
non-judgemental attitudes 65

obsessions 21–2, 24–5, 28–9, 31
about bad things happening to families 19–22, 83, *83*, 152–3, *153–4* 158
about dying 49–50, *51*
about school failure 74–5
common 22, *23*
definition 21, 27, 46
getting caught up in your child's 57
identifying your child's 55, *56*
identifying your own 46–7
measuring 62–4, 170
new 177
and the OCD trap 48, *48*, 49–50, *51–2* 53, 55
rating your 210–15
reality testing 25
recovery from 188
'reducing' the effects of by performing compulsions 21, 27, 28, 48, *48*, 50, *51–2*, 53, 74, 132, 146

and relapse 177, 178
resistant 165
and school 196, 197
which coincidently come true 166
see also unpleasant/intrusive thoughts
OCD action plans 119
for exposure and response prevention 89, *90*, 95–7, *97*, 99
for relapse 173, *175–6*, *180*
OCD diaries 59, 80–4, *82–3*
'OCD as illness' model 192–3
OCD ladders 59, 84–7, *86*, *88*, 92
and exposure and response prevention 84, 85, 89, 92, 95, 97, *97*, 99–100, *99*, 103, *104* 108, 110–11, 113–14, 116–18, 130, 158, 179
and behavioural experiments 161, 163, 164, 166
updating/re-rating 103, *104*, 108, 114
OCD rules, learning to break 96, *97*, 98–9
OCD timetables 62, *122–3*
OCD traps 22, 48–53, *48*, *51–2*, 55
OCD traps
and anxiety 75–6, *76*, 78
getting caught up in your child's 57

offending people, fear of
    49–50, *51*
'over-important' thoughts
    133–4, 141

parents and carers 18,
    28–30, 61–2, 65–8,
    92–3
  and anxiety 78–9, 194
  asking for help 193
  attention of 195
  and behavioural
      experiments 171–2
  children's unpleasant
      thoughts about
      19–22, 83, *83*, 152–3,
      153–4, 158
  and cognitive behaviour
      therapy 45
  and discipline 194–5
  and the effects of OCD
      on the family 192–5
  and exposure and
      response prevention
      108–9, 116–19,
      130–1
  guilt of 30, 192
  overcoming unhelpful
      thoughts and 146
  prioritising
      responsibilities 193
  pushing for change 130
  and the 'putting OCD on
      trial' technique 158
  and relapse 183
  and the responsibility
      pie-chart 158
  and self-care 193
  and sharing OCD
      experiences 192

shouting at children for
    performing rituals
    189
  support for 192, 193, 194
  supportive roles of 66–7
  and treatment 36–9
  understanding OCD
      55–8
  and discipline 194–5
  see also families
paroxetine 38
partners 195
perfectionism 130, 134,
    142, 146, 195
phobias 37
positive approaches 65–6
praise 108, 195
praying, compulsive 49–50,
    51
pressurising children 130
prevalence of OCD 22, 27,
    29, 31, 200
problem-solver role 66
progress, maintaining
    173–83
psychiatrists 18, 33
psychoanalysis 35
psychologists 18, 33
psychotherapy 35
'putting OCD on trial'
    technique 147–9,
    149–51, 157, 158

questionnaires, Children's
    Obsessive Compulsive
    Inventory (CHOCI)
    62–4, 170, 206–15

reality testing 25, 49, 50,
    60, 159–72

reassurance seeking
    113–14, 116, 118–19,
    124, 134, 189–90
recording OCD difficulties
    see OCD diaries
recovery 17, 188
  picturing 53
  see also treating OCD
referrals 15, 37, 38
relapse 66, 173–83, *175–6*,
    180
  identifying the symptoms
      of 177–8
  preventing with
      medication 39
  reasons for 174, 183
  tackling 173, *175–6*,
      178–81, *180*, 183
  and thinking about your
      goals 181–2
relationships 190
relaxation 35
repeating rituals 196–7
resistant symptoms 43
responsibility
  misconceived levels of
      (inflated) 133, 140,
      146, 152–7, *153–6*
  parental 193
responsibility pie-chart 147,
    152–7, *153–6*, 158, 166
reviewer role 67
risk factors for OCD 30,
    192
rituals *see* compulsions

school 196–8
  compulsions involving
      74–5, 77, 102, *102*
school counsellors 171–2

selective serotonin
  re-uptake inhibitors
  (SSRIs) 38, 39, 194
self-care 193
self-harm 38–9
serotonin 38
serotonin re-uptake
  inhibitors (SRIs) 16
sertraline 38
setbacks *see* relapse
severity scale of OCD
  14–16, 18
  and friends 198
  and treatment choice
    27–8
  see also measuring OCD
shame 28, 29
short obsessive compulsive
  scale (SOCS) *26*
siblings
  and parental attention
    195
  relationships with 190
  telling them about your
    OCD 188–9
  worrying they can catch
    your OCD 191
sickness, fears of 152–3,
  153–4, 160, 164, 166,
  171–2
spouses 195
SRIs *see* serotonin
  re-uptake inhibitors
SSRIs *see* selective
  serotonin re-uptake
  inhibitors
stress 174, 183
stress response 78
support
  for OCD kids 198,
    199–200

for parents and carers
  192, 193, 194
symptoms of OCD 22

taking charge of OCD
  139–40
talking treatments 16, 40
  see also cognitive
    behaviour therapy
Theory A or Theory B
  technique 148, *149–51*,
  158
therapists 18, 33, 197
thoughts
  'fighting' 144
  helpful 137–46, *138, 143*
  see also
    unpleasant/intrusive
    thoughts
threat, overestimation of
  72, 78
timetables, OCD 62, *122-3*
Tourette syndrome 37
treating OCD 13, 16–17,
  31–9
  effectiveness 34–5
  embarrassment about
    31–2
  getting help 31
  guidelines on 17, 18
  ineffective 35
  refusal 36
  and the severity of OCD
    27–8
  types of 34
  see also cognitive
    behaviour therapy;
    medication
treats 108

tummies, butterflies in your
  70

unacceptable behaviour,
  maintaining limits on
  194–5
uncertainty, dislike of 134,
  141–2, 146
unpleasant/intrusive
  thoughts 14–15, 19–22,
  24–5, 27–8, 31, 132–46
  about families 19–22, 83,
    83, 158
  belief in the
    over-importance of
    133–4, 141
  challenging and testing
    59–60, 137-46, *138,
    143*, 147–58, 166,
    168, 172
  not wanting to talk about
    158
  'putting OCD on trial'
    technique for 147–9,
    149–51, 157, 158
  replacing with helpful
    thoughts 137–46,
    138, 143
  resistance to exposure
    and response
    prevention 125–7
  responsibility pie-chart
    for 147, 152–7,
    153–6, 158
  role in OCD 132–46
  sexual content 146
  testing out 159–72
  typical 133–4, *135–6*, 146
  understanding your
    135–6

very strong 125–7
violent content 146
see also obsessions
unpredictable nature of
   OCD 173
upsetting people, fear of
   49–50, *51*

worry 29, 48–9
   cycle of 40, *41*
   learning to overcome 40,
      42
   ordinary childhood 37
   severe 59–60
   short-term relief of 48,
      53
   see also anxiety